ANGULAR SCATTERING FUNCTIONS
FOR SPHEROIDS

by Wilfried Heller / Masayuki Nakagaki / Gary D. Langolf

Wayne State University

Wayne State University Press / Detroit / 1972

1291403

Contents

For p = 1 see Tables indicated in reference 1.

Introduction and Acknowledgments

The Tables in this book are concerned with the scattering of electro-magnetic waves by dielectric, isotropic, non-absorbing bodies of nonspherical shape. The bodies are approximated by spheroids of widely varied axial ratio, the limiting shapes being those of a typical cylinder and of a typical disc respectively. While there has been a large number of Tables, many of them in book form, on light scattering functions of spherical scattering bodies,[1] the present Tables are the first to treat nonspherical scatterers systematically. They should therefore fill a definite need since a spherical shape is only one of the three basic regular shapes of matter. The data given are based upon a generalization[2] of a theory of A. F. Stevenson,[3] which in turn represents an extension of the Rayleigh[4]-Gans[5] theory on the scattering of nonspherical bodies of unrestricted relative refractive index.[6] In the Rayleigh-Gans theory,[6] the scattering bodies are assumed to be negligibly small compared to the wavelength of the electro-magnetic radiation incident upon them—just as in the original Rayleigh theory.[7] Consequently, they are treated again as dipole scatterers. In contradistinction to the latter theory, however, the induced dipole moment is assumed to be different along the symmetry axis of a spheroid and perpendicular to it. The extension of this theory, by Stevenson, takes into account also magnetic dipole and electric quadrupole radiation. The range of particle sizes which can be considered is therefore larger than on using the original Rayleigh-Gans theory. The Stevenson theory is limited to the intensity of scattering expected from randomly oriented spheroids on observing at 90° with respect to the direction of the primary beam. The generalized theory[2] considers also the variation of the scattered intensity with the angle of observation. This generalized theory should be applicable quantitatively up to the following maximal dimensions on using visible light:[8] length of rod-like objects of about 0.15 microns; diameter of disk-like objects of about 0.1 microns. In the case of radar waves, the maximum dimensions would be 0.25 mm and 0.2 mm, respectively. The former dimensions include both molecules of conventional size (molecular weight < 1000), rigid macromolecules and small colloidal particles. The Tables should allow one to determine the size (within the stated limits) and shape of nonspherical rigid scattering bodies, and the conformation of flexible bodies, particularly of low molecular weight compounds.

The Tables cover, in a comprehensive manner, the numerical variation of the intensity of laterally scattered radiation, e.g. light, with the angle of observation, for incident unpolarized light and for linearly polarized light of unit intensity whose electric vector is either parallel or perpendicular to the plane of observation. The values given for the intensity of laterally scattered light pertain both to the total intensity scattered at a given angle of observation and to the intensity of the components vibrating parallel and perpendicular respectively to the plane of observation. Possible practical application of these functions includes determination of the size and shape of solid or liquid pollutants in water or in air, whenever they are nonspherical in shape.

The authors are indebted to the late Dr. Walter Hoffman and to Dr. Charles F. Briggs of the Wayne State University Computing Center for making the facilities of the Center available and for assisting us in every way possible. The authors should also like to acknowledge the very helpful assistance received in connection with computational operations by Mr. Curtis Brock, Miss Catherine Chape, and Mr. John Mazay. The authors also wish to express their most sincere thanks to Dr. Harold Basilius, former Director, and Mr. Richard Kinney, Production Manager of the Wayne State University Press for their interest and help in making these data available in book form. Last, but not least, the authors would like to acknowledge the effective support received from the Office of Naval Research in connection with fundamental theoretical and experimental research on the size and shape of macromolecules and colloidal particles, carried out in this laboratory.

Definitions and Remarks on the Computer Program

A spheroid is defined dimensionally by the axial ratio:

$$p = a/b \tag{1}$$

where a is the semi-axis of symmetry and b is the length of the semi-transverse axis. Prolate spheroids (rod-like bodies) are characterized by $p > 1.0$, oblate spheroids (disc-like bodies) by $p < 1.0$. The quantity important for the theoretical treatment of scattering by a spheroid is its largest dimension relative to the wavelength in the medium. It is a in the case of prolate spheroids and (a/p) for oblate spheroids. Here,

$$\alpha = 2\pi a/\lambda = 2\pi a n_1/\lambda_o \tag{2}$$

where λ is the wavelength in the medium, λ_o that in the vacuum and n_1 is the refractive index of the medium. The primary dimensionless scattering function considered in the theory, whose numerical values are given in the present Tables, is

$$i_\theta = (2r\pi/\lambda)^2 J_\theta = (2\pi/\lambda)^2 \, J'_\theta. \tag{3}$$

J is the radiant energy scattered, from an incident beam of unit intensity, by a single particle which passes, at θ, per unit time and unit area through a differential surface element of a sphere of radius r. The scattering particle is located at the center of this sphere and it is assumed that its largest dimension is negligibly small compared to r. The quantity J'_θ represents the intensity of radiation scattered by a single particle per unit solid angle and per unit intensity of the incident beam, along a differential cone in the θ direction, θ being the angle of observation with respect to the direction of the incident beam. As apparent from its dimension, J' is the differential angular scattering cross section of a scattering body. For a dispersed system or solution containing N non-spherical bodies per cm^3 the intensity of radiation scattered by the unit volume of the system per unit solid angle for an incident beam of intensity $I_o{}^*$ is

$$I_\theta = NI_o J' \quad \text{ergs cm}^{-3}\text{sec}^{-1}. \tag{4}$$

Expressing the concentration in terms of c (g/100g), the specific intensity of radiation scattered per unit volume of the system and per unit solid angle is

$$\frac{R_\theta}{c} = \left(\frac{I}{I_o c}\right)_\theta = \frac{3\rho_{12}p^2}{2\lambda a^3 \rho_2} i_\theta \times 10^{-2} \tag{5}$$

Here, ρ_2 is the density of the scattering bodies and ρ_{12} that of the solution (dispersed system). On expressing the concentration in terms of g/ml

$$\frac{R_\theta}{c'} = \frac{3p^2}{2\lambda a^3 \rho_2} i_\theta. \tag{6}$$

---

*I_o has the dimension ergs cm^{-2} sec^{-1}. It therefore differs dimensionally from I_θ.

The present Tables give the numerical values of i as derived from the generalized Rayleigh-Gans-Stevenson (RGS) theory. The RGS equation, in its most general form, may be written

$$i = \overline{f}a^6 + \overline{g}a^8 + \dots \qquad (7)$$

where the first term represents the Rayleigh-Gans contribution to i and the second represents the Stevenson term. The numerical value of both $\overline{f}$ and $\overline{g}$ depends on eight variables so that the explicit expressions for i, given elsewhere[2,3] are rather complicated. Of these variables, three, viz., a, p and θ, have already been defined. The present Tables take into account also the effect of the following additional variables: (4) the refractive index of the scattering body (n_2) relative to that of the medium (n_1), viz., $m = (n_2/n_1)$; (5) the direction of vibration of an incident linearly polarized beam, relative to the plane of observation considering only the two practically most important directions, ∥ (parallel) and ⊥ (perpendicular) to the latter plane; and (6) the variation, in the intensity of the scattered beam, with the angle formed by the plane of polarization of an analyzing prism—placed between scattering system and observer—with the plane of observation, considering again only the angles of $0°$ (∥) and $90°$ (⊥) respectively. The last two variables (7) and (8) are the two angles which define the orientation of the symmetry axis of a spheroid, the angle it forms with the direction of the incident beam and with the plane of observation, respectively. The data given in the present Tables are the result of integration over all possible orientations of a spheroid with respect to the direction of the incident beam and the plane of observation and they apply therefore to a dispersed system (solution) at rest, in absence of any orienting torque. This averaging is expressed symbolically by the bar associated with f and g in equation (7).

The values of a, p and m considered are indicated in the Tables as parameters. For each of them, the variation, with θ, of SS, PP and SP is indicated. These symbols represent an abbreviation and modification, for technical reasons, of the scattering functions $i(\sigma,\sigma)$, $i(\pi,\pi)$ and $i(\sigma,\pi)$ respectively. Here, σ stands for perpendicular and π for parallel, in line with standard convention in molecular spectroscopy. The first symbol in the brackets indicates the orientation of the electric vector of an incident linearly polarized beam with respect to the plane of observation. The second symbol expresses the orientation, with respect to the same plane, of the plane of polarization of a polarizing prism which is interposed between scattering system and observer. The three entries indicated are sufficient since

$$i(\sigma,\pi) = i(\pi,\sigma) \qquad (8)$$

in a system containing randomly oriented spheroids.[9]

The Tables give not only information on the intensity of the four "Krishnan"—components[9] of scattering from spheroids, but in addition on the intensities of radiation scattered from an incident *unpolarized* beam (u) and on the *total* intensity scattered (t) of an incident polarized or unpolarized beam.

This follows from the simple relations:

$$i(\pi,\sigma) + i(\pi,\pi) = i(\pi,t) \tag{9}$$

$$i(\sigma,\sigma) + i(\sigma,\pi) = i(\sigma,t) \tag{10}$$

$$i(\pi,\sigma) + i(\sigma,\sigma) = 2i(u,\sigma) \tag{11}$$

$$i(\pi,\pi) + i(\sigma,\pi) = 2i(u,\pi) \tag{12}$$

$$i(u,\sigma) + i(u,\pi) = i(u,t) \tag{13}$$

The parameter values considered in the Tables are:

$\theta = 0, 5, 10(10), 40, 45, 50(10), 130, 135, 150, 165, 180°$

$m = 1.05, 1.10(0.10), 1.40$

$p = 50, 20, 10, 5, 2, 0.5, 0.2, 0.1$

$a_{p<1} = 0.02(0.02), 0.08$

$a_{p>1} = 0.1, 0.2(0.2), 1.0$

For technical reasons, θ and a are written out in the Tables, m is replaced by M and p by P.

The computations were carried out with the IBM 360, Model 65 using the Fortran IV programming system and floating point arithmetic of double precision. Since the functions involved are throughout monotonic, the problem of variance in the number of significant figures in the results such as it exists in the case of oscillatory functions (e.g., the Mie-scattering functions) does not exist here. The number of significant figures, therefore, is for all entries uniformly at least 5. The entries are given in accordance with accepted convention. Thus 0.81791 D-09 indicates 0.81791×10^{-9}.

References:

(1) H. Denman, W. Heller and W. J. Pangonis, *Angular Scattering Functions for Spheres,* Wayne State University Press, Detroit, Michigan (1966).

For a listing of earlier tables by both the present authors and other authors, see: M. Kerker, *The Scattering of Light and Other Electromagnetic Radiation,* Academic Press, New York, N.Y. (1969).

(2) W. Heller and M. Nakagaki, to be published elsewhere.

(3) A. F. Stevenson, J. Applied Physics, **24**, 1134, 1143 (1953).

(4) Lord Rayleigh, Phil. Mag. (5) **44**, 28 (1897); (6) **35**, 373 (1918).

(5) R. Gans, Ann. Physik (4) **37**, 881 (1912); **62**, 331 (1920).

(6) This Rayleigh-Gans theory is not to be confused with the more widely known Rayleigh-Gans theory dealing with the scattering of bodies of any shape whose refractive index is restricted by the requirement that it differs very little from that of the surrounding medium.

(7) Lord Rayleigh, see e.g., Phil. Mag. **12**, 81 (1881).

(8) According to a quantitative check of the prospective range of validity of the Stevenson equation, to be published elsewhere.

(9) R. S. Krishnan, Proc. Indian Acad. Sci., **Al**, 782 (1934); **A7**, 21 (1938); A. F. Stevenson, J. Applied Physics, **28**, 1015 (1957).

P = 50.00   M = 1.05

ALPHA = 0.10

THETA	SS	PP	SP
0.	0.17487D-15	0.17487D-15	0.29302D-19
5.	0.17487D-15	0.17354D-15	0.29302D-19
10.	0.17486D-15	0.16959D-15	0.29302D-19
20.	0.17485D-15	0.15439D-15	0.29301D-19
30.	0.17484D-15	0.13111D-15	0.29300D-19
40.	0.17481D-15	0.10256D-15	0.29299D-19
45.	0.17480D-15	0.87377D-16	0.29299D-19
50.	0.17479D-15	0.72198D-16	0.29298D-19
60.	0.17475D-15	0.43682D-16	0.29298D-19
70.	0.17472D-15	0.20448D-16	0.29298D-19
80.	0.17468D-15	0.52912D-17	0.29299D-19
90.	0.17464D-15	0.29284D-19	0.29301D-19
100.	0.17460D-15	0.52889D-17	0.29304D-19
110.	0.17456D-15	0.20430D-16	0.29308D-19
120.	0.17453D-15	0.43626D-16	0.29313D-19
130.	0.17450D-15	0.72078D-16	0.29318D-19
135.	0.17448D-15	0.87218D-16	0.29320D-19
150.	0.17445D-15	0.13081D-15	0.29327D-19
165.	0.17442D-15	0.16273D-15	0.29331D-19
180.	0.17442D-15	0.17442D-15	0.29333D-19

ALPHA = 0.20

THETA	SS	PP	SP
0.	0.11191D-13	0.11191D-13	0.18693D-17
5.	0.11190D-13	0.11105D-13	0.18692D-17
10.	0.11190D-13	0.10851D-13	0.18692D-17
20.	0.11187D-13	0.98747D-14	0.18690D-17
30.	0.11183D-13	0.83804D-14	0.18687D-17
40.	0.11177D-13	0.65504D-14	0.18684D-17
45.	0.11174D-13	0.55781D-14	0.18683D-17
50.	0.11170D-13	0.46069D-14	0.18681D-17
60.	0.11162D-13	0.27845D-14	0.18680D-17
70.	0.11153D-13	0.13022D-14	0.18680D-17
80.	0.11143D-13	0.33667D-15	0.18683D-17
90.	0.11133D-13	0.18646D-17	0.18689D-17
100.	0.11123D-13	0.33607D-15	0.18697D-17
110.	0.11113D-13	0.12976D-14	0.18707D-17
120.	0.11104D-13	0.27701D-14	0.18719D-17
130.	0.11096D-13	0.45762D-14	0.18732D-17
135.	0.11092D-13	0.55372D-14	0.18738D-17
150.	0.11083D-13	0.83053D-14	0.18755D-17
165.	0.11077D-13	0.10333D-13	0.18767D-17
180.	0.11075D-13	0.11075D-13	0.18771D-17

ALPHA = 0.40

THETA	SS	PP	SP
0.	0.71599D-12	0.71599D-12	0.11807D-15
5.	0.71594D-12	0.71042D-12	0.11807D-15
10.	0.71577D-12	0.69390D-12	0.11805D-15
20.	0.71510D-12	0.63043D-12	0.11800D-15
30.	0.71401D-12	0.53367D-12	0.11793D-15
40.	0.71253D-12	0.41576D-12	0.11785D-15
45.	0.71166D-12	0.35340D-12	0.11782D-15
50.	0.71071D-12	0.29130D-12	0.11778D-15
60.	0.70860D-12	0.17537D-12	0.11775D-15
70.	0.70626D-12	0.81690D-13	0.11776D-15
80.	0.70377D-12	0.21042D-13	0.11784D-15
90.	0.70120D-12	0.11688D-15	0.11798D-15
100.	0.69863D-12	0.20890D-13	0.11818D-15
110.	0.69614D-12	0.80511D-13	0.11845D-15
120.	0.69380D-12	0.17168D-12	0.11875D-15
130.	0.69169D-12	0.28345D-12	0.11908D-15
135.	0.69074D-12	0.34294D-12	0.11924D-15
150.	0.68839D-12	0.51446D-12	0.11967D-15
165.	0.68691D-12	0.64028D-12	0.11997D-15
180.	0.68640D-12	0.68640D-12	0.12008D-15

ALPHA = 0.60

THETA	SS	PP	SP
0.	0.81516D-11	0.81516D-11	0.13152D-14
5.	0.81502D-11	0.80863D-11	0.13151D-14
10.	0.81458D-11	0.78928D-11	0.13148D-14
20.	0.81287D-11	0.71516D-11	0.13135D-14
30.	0.81008D-11	0.60281D-11	0.13116D-14
40.	0.80629D-11	0.467C2D-11	0.13096D-14
45.	0.80405D-11	0.39571D-11	0.13087D-14
50.	0.80161D-11	0.32510D-11	0.13079D-14
60.	0.79620D-11	0.19436D-11	0.13070D-14
70.	0.79021D-11	0.89911D-12	0.13073D-14
80.	0.78383D-11	0.23011D-12	0.13092D-14
90.	0.77724D-11	0.12847D-14	0.13128D-14
100.	0.77066D-11	0.22621D-12	0.13182D-14
110.	0.76427D-11	0.86891D-12	0.13250D-14
120.	0.75828D-11	0.18490D-11	0.13328D-14
130.	0.75287D-11	0.30497D-11	0.13410D-14
135.	0.75043D-11	0.36892D-11	0.13451D-14
150.	0.74440D-11	0.55356D-11	0.13563D-14
165.	0.74062D-11	0.68942D-11	0.13640D-14
180.	0.73932D-11	0.73932D-11	0.13668D-14

P = 50.00   M = 1.05

ALPHA = 0.80

THETA	SS	PP	SP
0.	0.45769D-10	0.45769D-10	0.71565D-14
5.	0.45755D-10	0.45388D-10	0.71554D-14
10.	0.45712D-10	0.44259D-10	0.71520D-14
20.	0.45541D-10	0.39951D-10	0.71392D-14
30.	0.45262D-10	0.33470D-10	0.71207D-14
40.	0.44883D-10	0.25724D-10	0.71006D-14
45.	0.44660D-10	0.21696D-10	0.70913D-14
50.	0.44417D-10	0.17738D-10	0.70835D-14
60.	0.43876D-10	0.10496D-10	0.70744D-14
70.	0.43277D-10	0.48049D-11	0.70776D-14
80.	0.42640D-10	0.12176D-11	0.70965D-14
90.	0.41982D-10	0.68516D-14	0.71327D-14
100.	0.41324D-10	0.11787D-11	0.71859D-14
110.	0.40687D-10	0.45033D-11	0.72536D-14
120.	0.40088D-10	0.95508D-11	0.73317D-14
130.	0.39548D-10	0.15728D-10	0.74143D-14
135.	0.39304D-10	0.19020D-10	0.74552D-14
150.	0.38702D-10	0.28551D-10	0.75664D-14
165.	0.38324D-10	0.35598D-10	0.76436D-14
180.	0.38195D-10	0.38195D-10	0.76712D-14

ALPHA = 1.00

THETA	SS	PP	SP
0.	0.17444D-09	0.17444D-09	0.26156D-13
5.	0.17436D-09	0.17292D-09	0.26149D-13
10.	0.17410D-09	0.16841D-09	0.26129D-13
20.	0.17308D-09	0.15127D-09	0.26052D-13
30.	0.17142D-09	0.12572D-09	0.25942D-13
40.	0.16916D-09	0.95594D-10	0.25822D-13
45.	0.16783D-09	0.80129D-10	0.25767D-13
50.	0.16638D-09	0.65074D-10	0.25720D-13
60.	0.16315D-09	0.37957D-10	0.25666D-13
70.	0.15959D-09	0.17118D-10	0.25685D-13
80.	0.15579D-09	0.42751D-11	0.25798D-13
90.	0.15187D-09	0.24338D-13	0.26014D-13
100.	0.14795D-09	0.40434D-11	0.26331D-13
110.	0.14415D-09	0.15320D-10	0.26735D-13
120.	0.14058D-09	0.32324D-10	0.27200D-13
130.	0.13736D-09	0.53093D-10	0.27692D-13
135.	0.13590D-09	0.64176D-10	0.27936D-13
150.	0.13232D-09	0.96402D-10	0.28599D-13
165.	0.13006D-09	0.12040D-09	0.29059D-13
180.	0.12929D-09	0.12929D-09	0.29223D-13

3

ALPHA = 0.10

THETA	SS	PP	SP
0.	0.68838D-15	0.68838D-15	0.46721D-18
5.	0.68838D-15	0.68315D-15	0.46721D-18
10.	0.68837D-15	0.66761D-15	0.46721D-18
20.	0.68833D-15	0.60780D-15	0.46720D-18
30.	0.68826D-15	0.51621D-15	0.46718D-18
40.	0.68818D-15	0.40389D-15	0.46716D-18
45.	0.68813D-15	0.34415D-15	0.46715D-18
50.	0.68807D-15	0.28443D-15	0.46714D-18
60.	0.68795D-15	0.17223D-15	0.46713D-18
70.	0.68781D-15	0.80810D-16	0.46713D-18
80.	0.68767D-15	0.21171D-16	0.46714D-18
90.	0.68752D-15	0.46690D-18	0.46717D-18
100.	0.68737D-15	0.21163D-16	0.46722D-18
110.	0.68723D-15	0.80743D-16	0.46728D-18
120.	0.68709D-15	0.17201D-15	0.46735D-18
130.	0.68697D-15	0.28397D-15	0.46742D-18
135.	0.68691D-15	0.34354D-15	0.46746D-18
150.	0.68678D-15	0.51509D-15	0.46756D-18
165.	0.68669D-15	0.64069D-15	0.46764D-18
180.	0.68666D-15	0.68666D-15	0.46766D-18

ALPHA = 0.20

THETA	SS	PP	SP
0.	0.44050D-13	0.44050D-13	0.29809D-16
5.	0.44049D-13	0.43714D-13	0.29809D-16
10.	0.44047D-13	0.42715D-13	0.29808D-16
20.	0.44037D-13	0.38873D-13	0.29804D-16
30.	0.44021D-13	0.32995D-13	0.29799D-16
40.	0.43999D-13	0.25795D-13	0.29794D-16
45.	0.43986D-13	0.21970D-13	0.29791D-16
50.	0.43971D-13	0.18149D-13	0.29789D-16
60.	0.43940D-13	0.10979D-13	0.29786D-16
70.	0.43905D-13	0.51466D-14	0.29786D-16
80.	0.43868D-13	0.13472D-14	0.29790D-16
90.	0.43830D-13	0.29729D-16	0.29797D-16
100.	0.43792D-13	0.13450D-14	0.29809D-16
110.	0.43755D-13	0.51293D-14	0.29825D-16
120.	0.43720D-13	0.10925D-13	0.29843D-16
130.	0.43689D-13	0.18033D-13	0.29862D-16
135.	0.43674D-13	0.21815D-13	0.29872D-16
150.	0.43639D-13	0.32709D-13	0.29898D-16
165.	0.43617D-13	0.40688D-13	0.29916D-16
180.	0.43610D-13	0.43610D-13	0.29923D-16

ALPHA = 0.40

THETA	SS	PP	SP
0.	0.28176D-11	0.28176D-11	0.18840D-14
5.	0.28174D-11	0.27957D-11	0.18839D-14
10.	0.28167D-11	0.27307D-11	0.18837D-14
20.	0.28142D-11	0.24813D-11	0.18828D-14
30.	0.28100D-11	0.21008D-11	0.18815D-14
40.	0.28044D-11	0.16372D-11	0.18802D-14
45.	0.28011D-11	0.13919D-11	0.18795D-14
50.	0.27975D-11	0.11476D-11	0.18789D-14
60.	0.27894D-11	0.69154D-12	0.18781D-14
70.	0.27805D-11	0.32292D-12	0.18781D-14
80.	0.27710D-11	0.84223D-13	0.18791D-14
90.	0.27613D-11	0.18636D-14	0.18811D-14
100.	0.27515D-11	0.83682D-13	0.18841D-14
110.	0.27420D-11	0.31850D-12	0.18881D-14
120.	0.27331D-11	0.67757D-12	0.18927D-14
130.	0.27250D-11	0.11178D-11	0.18977D-14
135.	0.27214D-11	0.13521D-11	0.19002D-14
150.	0.27125D-11	0.20277D-11	0.19068D-14
165.	0.27068D-11	0.25233D-11	0.19115D-14
180.	0.27049D-11	0.27049D-11	0.19132D-14

ALPHA = 0.60

THETA	SS	PP	SP
0.	0.32064D-10	0.32064D-10	0.21008D-13
5.	0.32058D-10	0.31807D-10	0.21006D-13
10.	0.32042D-10	0.31047D-10	0.21000D-13
20.	0.31977D-10	0.28137D-10	0.20978D-13
30.	0.31870D-10	0.23724D-10	0.20946D-13
40.	0.31726D-10	0.18388D-10	0.20910D-13
45.	0.31641D-10	0.15585D-10	0.20893D-13
50.	0.31548D-10	0.12808D-10	0.20878D-13
60.	0.31342D-10	0.76659D-11	0.20859D-13
70.	0.31114D-10	0.35555D-11	0.20858D-13
80.	0.30871D-10	0.92148D-12	0.20882D-13
90.	0.30620D-10	0.20485D-13	0.20934D-13
100.	0.30369D-10	0.90762D-12	0.21012D-13
110.	0.30126D-10	0.34422D-11	0.21114D-13
120.	0.29898D-10	0.73078D-11	0.21233D-13
130.	0.29692D-10	0.12044D-10	0.21360D-13
135.	0.29599D-10	0.14566D-10	0.21423D-13
150.	0.29369D-10	0.21849D-10	0.21594D-13
165.	0.29225D-10	0.27208D-10	0.21714D-13
180.	0.29176D-10	0.29176D-10	0.21757D-13

P = 50.00   M = 1.10

ALPHA = 0.80

THETA	SS	PP	SP
0.	0.17992D-09	0.17992D-09	0.11448D-12
5.	0.17986D-09	0.17842D-09	0.11446D-12
10.	0.17970D-09	0.17399D-09	0.11440D-12
20.	0.17905D-09	0.15710D-09	0.11418D-12
30.	0.17798D-09	0.13167D-09	0.11386D-12
40.	0.17654D-09	0.10126D-09	0.11351D-12
45.	0.17569D-09	0.85443D-10	0.11334D-12
50.	0.17476D-09	0.69888D-10	0.11319D-12
60.	0.17270D-09	0.41411D-10	0.11299D-12
70.	0.17043D-09	0.19012D-10	0.11299D-12
80.	0.16800D-09	0.48796D-11	0.11323D-12
90.	0.16549D-09	0.10926D-12	0.11374D-12
100.	0.16299D-09	0.47411D-11	0.11452D-12
110.	0.16056D-09	0.17880D-10	0.11554D-12
120.	0.15828D-09	0.37834D-10	0.11673D-12
130.	0.15622D-09	0.62255D-10	0.11800D-12
135.	0.15529D-09	0.75271D-10	0.11863D-12
150.	0.15300D-09	0.11295D-09	0.12034D-12
165.	0.15156D-09	0.14081D-09	0.12153D-12
180.	0.15107D-09	0.15107D-09	0.12196D-12

ALPHA = 1.00

THETA	SS	PP	SP
0.	0.68515D-09	0.68515D-09	0.41929D-12
5.	0.68482D-09	0.67918D-09	0.41917D-12
10.	0.68384D-09	0.66152D-09	0.41882D-12
20.	0.67996D-09	0.59442D-09	0.41751D-12
30.	0.67363D-09	0.49435D-09	0.41560D-12
40.	0.66503D-09	0.37622D-09	0.41347D-12
45.	0.65997D-09	0.31553D-09	0.41246D-12
50.	0.65444D-09	0.25642D-09	0.41157D-12
60.	0.64216D-09	0.14982D-09	0.41040D-12
70.	0.62858D-09	0.67788D-10	0.41037D-12
80.	0.61411D-09	0.17153D-10	0.41180D-12
90.	0.59918D-09	0.38815D-12	0.41486D-12
100.	0.58425D-09	0.16327D-10	0.41954D-12
110.	0.56978D-09	0.61043D-10	0.42561D-12
120.	0.55620D-09	0.12850D-09	0.43269D-12
130.	0.54392D-09	0.21092D-09	0.44023D-12
135.	0.53839D-09	0.25490D-09	0.44398D-12
150.	0.52473D-09	0.38277D-09	0.45420D-12
165.	0.51614D-09	0.47797D-09	0.46132D-12
180.	0.51322D-09	0.51322D-09	0.46387D-12

ALPHA = 0.10

THETA	SS	PP	SP
0.	0.26732D-14	0.26732D-14	0.73843D-17
5.	0.26732D-14	0.26529D-14	0.73843D-17
10.	0.26731D-14	0.25927D-14	0.73842D-17
20.	0.26730D-14	0.23610D-14	0.73840D-17
30.	0.26728D-14	0.20060D-14	0.73836D-17
40.	0.26725D-14	0.15708D-14	0.73832D-17
45.	0.26723D-14	0.13393D-14	0.73830D-17
50.	0.26721D-14	0.11078D-14	0.73829D-17
60.	0.26716D-14	0.67303D-15	0.73826D-17
70.	0.26711D-14	0.31875D-15	0.73825D-17
80.	0.26706D-14	0.87617D-16	0.73826D-17
90.	0.26701D-14	0.73788D-17	0.73830D-17
100.	0.26695D-14	0.87595D-16	0.73837D-17
110.	0.26690D-14	0.31852D-15	0.73845D-17
120.	0.26685D-14	0.67227D-15	0.73856D-17
130.	0.26681D-14	0.11062D-14	0.73867D-17
135.	0.26679D-14	0.13371D-14	0.73872D-17
150.	0.26674D-14	0.20020D-14	0.73888D-17
165.	0.26670D-14	0.24888D-14	0.73898D-17
180.	0.26669D-14	0.26669D-14	0.73902D-17

ALPHA = 0.20

THETA	SS	PP	SP
0.	0.17104D-12	0.17104D-12	0.47124D-15
5.	0.17104D-12	0.16974D-12	0.47123D-15
10.	0.17103D-12	0.16587D-12	0.47122D-15
20.	0.17099D-12	0.15099D-12	0.47116D-15
30.	0.17093D-12	0.12821D-12	0.47107D-15
40.	0.17085D-12	0.10032D-12	0.47097D-15
45.	0.17080D-12	0.85497D-13	0.47092D-15
50.	0.17075D-12	0.70690D-13	0.47088D-15
60.	0.17064D-12	0.42906D-13	0.47081D-15
70.	0.17051D-12	0.20302D-13	0.47078D-15
80.	0.17038D-12	0.55758D-14	0.47082D-15
90.	0.17024D-12	0.46984D-15	0.47092D-15
100.	0.17010D-12	0.55701D-14	0.47108D-15
110.	0.16997D-12	0.20243D-13	0.47130D-15
120.	0.16984D-12	0.42712D-13	0.47157D-15
130.	0.16973D-12	0.70272D-13	0.47185D-15
135.	0.16967D-12	0.84937D-13	0.47199D-15
150.	0.16955D-12	0.12718D-12	0.47238D-15
165.	0.16947D-12	0.15811D-12	0.47266D-15
180.	0.16944D-12	0.16944D-12	0.47276D-15

ALPHA = 0.40

THETA	SS	PP	SP
0.	0.10935D-10	0.10935D-10	0.29812D-13
5.	0.10934D-10	0.10850D-10	0.29811D-13
10.	0.10932D-10	0.10599D-10	0.29807D-13
20.	0.10922D-10	0.96334D-11	0.29792D-13
30.	0.10907D-10	0.81610D-11	0.29769D-13
40.	0.10887D-10	0.63661D-11	0.29744D-13
45.	0.10875D-10	0.54163D-11	0.29731D-13
50.	0.10862D-10	0.44702D-11	0.29719D-13
60.	0.10832D-10	0.27031D-11	0.29702D-13
70.	0.10800D-10	0.12742D-11	0.29696D-13
80.	0.10766D-10	0.34874D-12	0.29705D-13
90.	0.10730D-10	0.29453D-13	0.29730D-13
100.	0.10695D-10	0.34728D-12	0.29772D-13
110.	0.10660D-10	0.12591D-11	0.29829D-13
120.	0.10628D-10	0.26535D-11	0.29896D-13
130.	0.10599D-10	0.43631D-11	0.29969D-13
135.	0.10586D-10	0.52731D-11	0.30005D-13
150.	0.10553D-10	0.78962D-11	0.30105D-13
165.	0.10533D-10	0.98204D-11	0.30175D-13
180.	0.10526D-10	0.10526D-10	0.30201D-13

ALPHA = 0.60

THETA	SS	PP	SP
0.	0.12433D-09	0.12433D-09	0.33300D-12
5.	0.12431D-09	0.12334D-09	0.33296D-12
10.	0.12425D-09	0.12041D-09	0.33286D-12
20.	0.12401D-09	0.10917D-09	0.33247D-12
30.	0.12363D-09	0.92115D-10	0.33189D-12
40.	0.12310D-09	0.71484D-10	0.33123D-12
45.	0.12280D-09	0.60640D-10	0.33091D-12
50.	0.12246D-09	0.49893D-10	0.33061D-12
60.	0.12171D-09	0.29975D-10	0.33017D-12
70.	0.12088D-09	0.14038D-10	0.33001D-12
80.	0.12000D-09	0.38183D-11	0.33023D-12
90.	0.11909D-09	0.32379D-12	0.33088D-12
100.	0.11818D-09	0.37809D-11	0.33196D-12
110.	0.11730D-09	0.13650D-10	0.33341D-12
120.	0.11647D-09	0.28703D-10	0.33514D-12
130.	0.11572D-09	0.47148D-10	0.33701D-12
135.	0.11538D-09	0.56970D-10	0.33794D-12
150.	0.11455D-09	0.85328D-10	0.34051D-12
165.	0.11402D-09	0.10615D-09	0.34230D-12
180.	0.11385D-09	0.11385D-09	0.34295D-12

ALPHA = 0.80

THETA	SS	PP	SP
0.	0.69682D-09	0.69682D-09	0.18192D-11
5.	0.69662D-09	0.69107D-09	0.18189D-11
10.	0.69602D-09	0.67402D-09	0.18178D-11
20.	0.69366D-09	0.60895D-09	0.18139D-11
30.	0.68980D-09	0.51092D-09	0.18082D-11
40.	0.68457D-09	0.39354D-09	0.18016D-11
45.	0.68148D-09	0.33242D-09	0.17983D-11
50.	0.67811D-09	0.27227D-09	0.17954D-11
60.	0.67064D-09	0.16201D-09	0.17909D-11
70.	0.66237D-09	0.75132D-10	0.17893D-11
80.	0.65355D-09	0.20242D-10	0.17916D-11
90.	0.64446D-09	0.17272D-11	0.17981D-11
100.	0.63536D-09	0.19868D-10	0.18088D-11
110.	0.62655D-09	0.71255D-10	0.18233D-11
120.	0.61828D-09	0.14931D-09	0.18406D-11
130.	0.61080D-09	0.24485D-09	0.18593D-11
135.	0.60743D-09	0.29576D-09	0.18686D-11
150.	0.59911D-09	0.44313D-09	0.18942D-11
165.	0.59388D-09	0.55200D-09	0.19121D-11
180.	0.59209D-09	0.59209D-09	0.19186D-11

ALPHA = 1.00

THETA	SS	PP	SP
0.	0.26496D-08	0.26496D-08	0.66857D-11
5.	0.26484D-08	0.26267D-08	0.66836D-11
10.	0.26448D-08	0.25589D-08	0.66774D-11
20.	0.26307D-08	0.23012D-08	0.66541D-11
30.	0.26078D-08	0.19164D-08	0.66198D-11
40.	0.25765D-08	0.14615D-08	0.65805D-11
45.	0.25582D-08	0.12274D-08	0.65613D-11
50.	0.25381D-08	0.99909D-09	0.65437D-11
60.	0.24935D-08	0.58659D-09	0.65171D-11
70.	0.24442D-08	0.26824D-09	0.65077D-11
80.	0.23917D-08	0.71275D-10	0.65209D-11
90.	0.23375D-08	0.61374D-11	0.65596D-11
100.	0.22833D-08	0.69046D-10	0.66238D-11
110.	0.22307D-08	0.24513D-09	0.67103D-11
120.	0.21814D-08	0.51088D-09	0.68132D-11
130.	0.21368D-08	0.83563D-09	0.69244D-11
135.	0.21168D-08	0.10089D-08	0.69801D-11
150.	0.20672D-08	0.15123D-08	0.71327D-11
165.	0.20360D-08	0.18868D-08	0.72396D-11
180.	0.20254D-08	0.20254D-08	0.72779D-11

ALPHA = 0.10

THETA	SS	PP	SP
0.	0.58629D-14	0.58629D-14	0.36727D-16
5.	0.58629D-14	0.58186D-14	0.36726D-16
10.	0.58629D-14	0.56870D-14	0.36726D-16
20.	0.58626D-14	0.51806D-14	0.36725D-16
30.	0.58621D-14	0.44049D-14	0.36723D-16
40.	0.58615D-14	0.34537D-14	0.36721D-16
45.	0.58611D-14	0.29477D-14	0.36720D-16
50.	0.58607D-14	0.24419D-14	0.36719D-16
60.	0.58598D-14	0.14916D-14	0.36717D-16
70.	0.58587D-14	0.71725D-15	0.36716D-16
80.	0.58577D-14	0.21207D-15	0.36717D-16
90.	0.58566D-14	0.36697D-16	0.36718D-16
100.	0.58554D-14	0.21205D-15	0.36721D-16
110.	0.58544D-14	0.71682D-15	0.36725D-16
120.	0.58534D-14	0.14901D-14	0.36730D-16
130.	0.58525D-14	0.24386D-14	0.36735D-16
135.	0.58520D-14	0.29433D-14	0.36737D-16
150.	0.58510D-14	0.43966D-14	0.36745D-16
165.	0.58504D-14	0.54607D-14	0.36750D-16
180.	0.58502D-14	0.58502D-14	0.36752D-16

ALPHA = 0.20

THETA	SS	PP	SP
0.	0.37509D-12	0.37509D-12	0.23442D-14
5.	0.37508D-12	0.37224D-12	0.23442D-14
10.	0.37506D-12	0.36379D-12	0.23441D-14
20.	0.37499D-12	0.33127D-12	0.23438D-14
30.	0.37487D-12	0.28151D-12	0.23433D-14
40.	0.37470D-12	0.22056D-12	0.23427D-14
45.	0.37461D-12	0.18818D-12	0.23425D-14
50.	0.37450D-12	0.15582D-12	0.23422D-14
60.	0.37427D-12	0.95093D-13	0.23418D-14
70.	0.37401D-12	0.45686D-13	0.23416D-14
80.	0.37373D-12	0.13497D-13	0.23417D-14
90.	0.37345D-12	0.23367D-14	0.23420D-14
100.	0.37317D-12	0.13491D-13	0.23428D-14
110.	0.37289D-12	0.45576D-13	0.23438D-14
120.	0.37263D-12	0.94710D-13	0.23450D-14
130.	0.37240D-12	0.15497D-12	0.23463D-14
135.	0.37229D-12	0.18704D-12	0.23470D-14
150.	0.37203D-12	0.27940D-12	0.23489D-14
165.	0.37187D-12	0.34705D-12	0.23502D-14
180.	0.37181D-12	0.37181D-12	0.23506D-14

P = 50.00   M = 1.30

ALPHA = 0.40

THETA	SS	PP	SP
0.	0.23969D-10	0.23969D-10	0.14842D-12
5.	0.23967D-10	0.23784D-10	0.14841D-12
10.	0.23963D-10	0.23236D-10	0.14839D-12
20.	0.23944D-10	0.21129D-10	0.14831D-12
30.	0.23913D-10	0.17915D-10	0.14819D-12
40.	0.23871D-10	0.13995D-10	0.14804D-12
45.	0.23846D-10	0.11921D-10	0.14797D-12
50.	0.23819D-10	0.98536D-11	0.14791D-12
60.	0.23760D-10	0.59919D-11	0.14780D-12
70.	0.23693D-10	0.28682D-11	0.14775D-12
80.	0.23623D-10	0.84441D-12	0.14776D-12
90.	0.23550D-10	0.14649D-12	0.14787D-12
100.	0.23478D-10	0.84295D-12	0.14805D-12
110.	0.23407D-10	0.28400D-11	0.14831D-12
120.	0.23341D-10	0.58937D-11	0.14862D-12
130.	0.23281D-10	0.96378D-11	0.14896D-12
135.	0.23254D-10	0.11631D-10	0.14914D-12
150.	0.23188D-10	0.17375D-10	0.14961D-12
165.	0.23146D-10	0.21587D-10	0.14994D-12
180.	0.23131D-10	0.23131D-10	0.15006D-12

ALPHA = 0.60

THETA	SS	PP	SP
0.	0.27233D-09	0.27233D-09	0.16600D-11
5.	0.27229D-09	0.27017D-09	0.16598D-11
10.	0.27217D-09	0.26378D-09	0.16593D-11
20.	0.27168D-09	0.23929D-09	0.16572D-11
30.	0.27089D-09	0.20212D-09	0.16540D-11
40.	0.26982D-09	0.15712D-09	0.16504D-11
45.	0.26919D-09	0.13345D-09	0.16486D-11
50.	0.26850D-09	0.10959D-09	0.16469D-11
60.	0.26696D-09	0.66465D-10	0.16441D-11
70.	0.26527D-09	0.31614D-10	0.16428D-11
80.	0.26346D-09	0.92504D-11	0.16432D-11
90.	0.26160D-09	0.16106D-11	0.16458D-11
100.	0.25973D-09	0.92131D-11	0.16506D-11
110.	0.25793D-09	0.30890D-10	0.16572D-11
120.	0.25623D-09	0.63949D-10	0.16652D-11
130.	0.25470D-09	0.10445D-09	0.16740D-11
135.	0.25401D-09	0.12602D-09	0.16784D-11
150.	0.25230D-09	0.18828D-09	0.16906D-11
165.	0.25123D-09	0.23406D-09	0.16991D-11
180.	0.25086D-09	0.25086D-09	0.17022D-11

ALPHA = 0.80

THETA	SS	PP	SP
0.	0.15247D-08	0.15247D-08	0.90866D-11
5.	0.15243D-08	0.15122D-08	0.90848D-11
10.	0.15230D-08	0.14751D-08	0.90792D-11
20.	0.15182D-08	0.13337D-08	0.90581D-11
30.	0.15103D-08	0.11204D-08	0.90268D-11
40.	0.14996D-08	0.86476D-09	0.89904D-11
45.	0.14933D-08	0.73150D-09	0.89722D-11
50.	0.14864D-08	0.60025D-09	0.89552D-11
60.	0.14711D-08	0.35939D-09	0.89278D-11
70.	0.14541D-08	0.16931D-09	0.89142D-11
80.	0.14361D-08	0.49081D-10	0.89191D-11
90.	0.14175D-08	0.85928D-11	0.89450D-11
100.	0.13989D-08	0.48708D-10	0.89922D-11
110.	0.13808D-08	0.16208D-09	0.90583D-11
120.	0.13639D-08	0.33426D-09	0.91384D-11
130.	0.13486D-08	0.54499D-09	0.92260D-11
135.	0.13417D-08	0.65727D-09	0.92701D-11
150.	0.13246D-08	0.98211D-09	0.93917D-11
165.	0.13139D-08	0.12220D-08	0.94772D-11
180.	0.13103D-08	0.13103D-08	0.95080D-11

ALPHA = 1.00

THETA	SS	PP	SP
0.	0.57894D-08	0.57894D-08	0.33484D-10
5.	0.57870D-08	0.57398D-08	0.33472D-10
10.	0.57797D-08	0.55930D-08	0.33439D-10
20.	0.57509D-08	0.50343D-08	0.33314D-10
30.	0.57038D-08	0.41993D-08	0.33127D-10
40.	0.56399D-08	0.32103D-08	0.32910D-10
45.	0.56023D-08	0.27006D-08	0.32801D-10
50.	0.55612D-08	0.22029D-08	0.32700D-10
60.	0.54699D-08	0.13021D-08	0.32537D-10
70.	0.53690D-08	0.60505D-09	0.32456D-10
80.	0.52614D-08	0.17303D-09	0.32485D-10
90.	0.51504D-08	0.30540D-10	0.32639D-10
100.	0.50395D-08	0.17081D-09	0.32921D-10
110.	0.49319D-08	0.56197D-09	0.33314D-10
120.	0.48309D-08	0.11523D-08	0.33792D-10
130.	0.47397D-08	0.18735D-08	0.34314D-10
135.	0.46986D-08	0.22581D-08	0.34577D-10
150.	0.45971D-08	0.33749D-08	0.35302D-10
165.	0.45332D-08	0.42047D-08	0.35811D-10
180.	0.45115D-08	0.45115D-08	0.35995D-10

ALPHA = 0.10

THETA	SS	PP	SP
0.	0.10208D-13	0.10208D-13	0.11359D-15
5.	0.10208D-13	0.10132D-13	0.11359D-15
10.	0.10208D-13	0.99037D-14	0.11359D-15
20.	0.10208D-13	0.90263D-14	0.11359D-15
30.	0.10207D-13	0.76823D-14	0.11358D-15
40.	0.10206D-13	0.60342D-14	0.11358D-15
45.	0.10205D-13	0.51575D-14	0.11357D-15
50.	0.10205D-13	0.42811D-14	0.11357D-15
60.	0.10203D-13	0.26345D-14	0.11356D-15
70.	0.10202D-13	0.12927D-14	0.11356D-15
80.	0.10200D-13	0.41737D-15	0.11356D-15
90.	0.10198D-13	0.11350D-15	0.11356D-15
100.	0.10196D-13	0.41738D-15	0.11357D-15
110.	0.10195D-13	0.12921D-14	0.11358D-15
120.	0.10193D-13	0.26321D-14	0.11360D-15
130.	0.10191D-13	0.42758D-14	0.11361D-15
135.	0.10191D-13	0.51505D-14	0.11362D-15
150.	0.10189D-13	0.76689D-14	0.11364D-15
165.	0.10188D-13	0.95128D-14	0.11366D-15
180.	0.10188D-13	0.10188D-13	0.11366D-15

ALPHA = 0.20

THETA	SS	PP	SP
0.	0.65303D-12	0.65303D-12	0.72517D-14
5.	0.65302D-12	0.64810D-12	0.72517D-14
10.	0.65299D-12	0.63346D-12	0.72514D-14
20.	0.65287D-12	0.57714D-12	0.72503D-14
30.	0.65267D-12	0.49094D-12	0.72487D-14
40.	0.65241D-12	0.38535D-12	0.72469D-14
45.	0.65225D-12	0.32924D-12	0.72459D-14
50.	0.65208D-12	0.27318D-12	0.72451D-14
60.	0.65170D-12	0.16796D-12	0.72436D-14
70.	0.65128D-12	0.82347D-13	0.72427D-14
80.	0.65084D-12	0.26564D-13	0.72427D-14
90.	0.65037D-12	0.72271D-14	0.72437D-14
100.	0.64991D-12	0.26567D-13	0.72457D-14
110.	0.64947D-12	0.82190D-13	0.72486D-14
120.	0.64905D-12	0.16737D-12	0.72521D-14
130.	0.64867D-12	0.27184D-12	0.72561D-14
135.	0.64850D-12	0.32743D-12	0.72581D-14
150.	0.64808D-12	0.48753D-12	0.72636D-14
165.	0.64781D-12	0.60479D-12	0.72675D-14
180.	0.64772D-12	0.64772D-12	0.72689D-14

ALPHA = 0.40

THETA	SS	PP	SP
0.	0.41713D-10	0.41713D-10	0.45942D-12
5.	0.41711D-10	0.41394D-10	0.45940D-12
10.	0.41703D-10	0.40444D-10	0.45933D-12
20.	0.41672D-10	0.36759D-10	0.45905D-12
30.	0.41622D-10	0.31235D-10	0.45865D-12
40.	0.41554D-10	0.24449D-1C	0.45818D-12
45.	0.41514D-10	0.20856D-10	0.45794D-12
50.	0.41471D-10	0.17276D-10	0.45771D-12
60.	0.41374D-10	0.10585D-1C	0.45733D-12
70.	0.41266D-10	0.51710D-11	0.45711D-12
80.	0.41152D-10	0.16624D-11	0.45711D-12
90.	0.41034D-10	0.45310D-12	0.45736D-12
100.	0.40916D-10	0.16632D-11	0.45787D-12
110.	0.40801D-10	0.51307D-11	0.45861D-12
120.	0.40694D-10	0.10433D-1C	0.45952D-12
130.	0.40597D-10	0.16933D-10	0.46053D-12
135.	0.40553D-10	0.20392D-10	0.46104D-12
150.	0.40445D-10	0.30363D-1C	0.46245D-12
165.	0.40378D-10	0.37675D-10	0.46345D-12
180.	0.40354D-10	0.40354D-10	0.46381D-12

ALPHA = 0.60

THETA	SS	PP	SP
0.	0.47361D-09	0.47361D-09	0.51440D-11
5.	0.47354D-09	0.46989D-09	0.51434D-11
10.	0.47335D-09	0.45885D-09	0.51416D-11
20.	0.47256D-09	0.41653D-09	0.51346D-11
30.	0.47128D-09	0.35228D-09	0.51243D-11
40.	0.46954D-09	0.27444D-09	0.51121D-11
45.	0.46851D-09	0.23348D-09	0.51060D-11
50.	0.46739D-09	0.19284D-09	0.51001D-11
60.	0.46490D-09	0.11744D-09	0.50903D-11
70.	0.46215D-09	0.57016D-10	0.50847D-11
80.	0.45922D-09	0.18220D-10	0.50847D-11
90.	0.45620D-09	0.49821D-11	0.50912D-11
100.	0.45317D-09	0.18240D-10	0.51043D-11
110.	0.45024D-09	0.55984D-10	0.51232D-11
120.	0.44749D-09	0.11354D-09	0.51466D-11
130.	0.44501D-09	0.18405D-09	0.51724D-11
135.	0.44389D-09	0.22159D-09	0.51855D-11
150.	0.44112D-09	0.32992D-09	0.52217D-11
165.	0.43938D-09	0.40955D-09	0.52473D-11
180.	0.43879D-09	0.43879D-09	0.52566D-11

P = 50.00   M = 1.40

ALPHA = 0.80

THETA	SS	PP	SP
0.	0.26490D-08	0.26490D-08	0.28202D-10
5.	0.26484D-08	0.26275D-08	0.28196D-10
10.	0.26464D-08	0.25636D-08	0.28177D-10
20.	0.26385D-08	0.23197D-08	0.28108D-10
30.	0.26257D-08	0.19517D-08	0.28005D-10
40.	0.26083D-08	0.15101D-08	0.27883D-10
45.	0.25981D-08	0.12797D-08	0.27822D-10
50.	0.25869D-08	0.10525D-08	0.27763D-10
60.	0.25621D-08	0.63529D-09	0.27666D-10
70.	0.25346D-08	0.30553D-09	0.27610D-10
80.	0.25053D-08	0.96745D-10	0.27610D-10
90.	0.24751D-08	0.26585D-10	0.27674D-10
100.	0.24449D-08	0.96937D-10	0.27805D-10
110.	0.24156D-08	0.29522D-09	0.27994D-10
120.	0.23881D-08	0.59629D-09	0.28228D-10
130.	0.23633D-08	0.96467D-09	0.28486D-10
135.	0.23521D-08	0.11609D-08	0.28617D-10
150.	0.23245D-08	0.17284D-08	0.28978D-10
165.	0.23071D-08	0.21471D-08	0.29234D-10
180.	0.23012D-08	0.23012D-08	0.29326D-10

ALPHA = 1.00

THETA	SS	PP	SP
0.	0.10046D-07	0.10046D-07	0.10414D-09
5.	0.10042D-07	0.99610D-08	0.10411D-09
10.	0.10030D-07	0.97085D-08	0.10400D-09
20.	0.99837D-08	0.87477D-08	0.10359D-09
30.	0.99074D-08	0.73098D-08	0.10297D-09
40.	0.98037D-08	0.56041D-08	0.10225D-09
45.	0.97426D-08	0.47238D-08	0.10188D-09
50.	0.96759D-08	0.38632D-08	0.10153D-09
60.	0.95279D-08	0.23029D-08	0.10095D-09
70.	0.93641D-08	0.10928D-08	0.10062D-09
80.	0.91896D-08	0.34145D-09	0.10062D-09
90.	0.90095D-08	0.94507D-10	0.10100D-09
100.	0.88295D-08	0.34259D-09	0.10178D-09
110.	0.86550D-08	0.10314D-08	0.10291D-09
120.	0.84912D-08	0.20704D-08	0.10430D-09
130.	0.83432D-08	0.33394D-08	0.10584D-09
135.	0.82765D-08	0.40159D-08	0.10662D-09
150.	0.81117D-08	0.59785D-08	0.10877D-09
165.	0.80082D-08	0.74348D-08	0.11030D-09
180.	0.79728D-08	0.79728D-08	0.11085D-09

15

ALPHA = 0.10

THETA	SS	PP	SP
0.	0.68305D-14	0.68305D-14	0.11077D-17
5.	0.68305D-14	0.67785D-14	0.11077D-17
10.	0.68304D-14	0.66243D-14	0.11077D-17
20.	0.68300D-14	0.60305D-14	0.11077D-17
30.	0.68293D-14	0.51211D-14	0.11076D-17
40.	0.68284D-14	0.40061D-14	0.11076D-17
45.	0.68279D-14	0.34130D-14	0.11076D-17
50.	0.68273D-14	0.28201D-14	0.11076D-17
60.	0.68261D-14	0.17062D-14	0.11075D-17
70.	0.68247D-14	0.79870D-15	0.11075D-17
80.	0.68232D-14	0.20664D-15	0.11076D-17
90.	0.68216D-14	0.11070D-17	0.11077D-17
100.	0.68201D-14	0.20655D-15	0.11078D-17
110.	0.68186D-14	0.79799D-15	0.11080D-17
120.	0.68172D-14	0.17040D-14	0.11081D-17
130.	0.68159D-14	0.28154D-14	0.11083D-17
135.	0.68154D-14	0.34068D-14	0.11084D-17
150.	0.68140D-14	0.51096D-14	0.11087D-17
165.	0.68131D-14	0.63564D-14	0.11088D-17
180.	0.68128D-14	0.68128D-14	0.11089D-17

ALPHA = 0.20

THETA	SS	PP	SP
0.	0.43713D-12	0.43713D-12	0.70667D-16
5.	0.43712D-12	0.43379D-12	0.70666D-16
10.	0.43709D-12	0.42387D-12	0.70664D-16
20.	0.43699D-12	0.38572D-12	0.70657D-16
30.	0.43682D-12	0.32735D-12	0.70647D-16
40.	0.43659D-12	0.25587D-12	0.70636D-16
45.	0.43646D-12	0.21789D-12	0.70631D-16
50.	0.43632D-12	0.17995D-12	0.70627D-16
60.	0.43599D-12	0.10877D-12	0.70622D-16
70.	0.43563D-12	0.50865D-13	0.70625D-16
80.	0.43525D-12	0.13148D-13	0.70636D-16
90.	0.43486D-12	0.70496D-16	0.70658D-16
100.	0.43446D-12	0.13125D-13	0.70690D-16
110.	0.43408D-12	0.50684D-13	0.70730D-16
120.	0.43372D-12	0.10820D-12	0.70775D-16
130.	0.43340D-12	0.17874D-12	0.70824D-16
135.	0.43325D-12	0.21628D-12	0.70847D-16
150.	0.43289D-12	0.32440D-12	0.70912D-16
165.	0.43266D-12	0.40359D-12	0.70957D-16
180.	0.43259D-12	0.43259D-12	0.70973D-16

ALPHA = 0.40

THETA	SS	PP	SP
0.	0.27969D-10	0.27969D-10	0.44647D-14
5.	0.27967D-10	0.27752D-10	0.44645D-14
10.	0.27961D-10	0.27106D-10	0.44640D-14
20.	0.27934D-10	0.24627D-10	0.44622D-14
30.	0.27892D-10	0.20847D-10	0.44596D-14
40.	0.27833D-10	0.16241D-10	0.44567D-14
45.	0.27799D-10	0.13805D-10	0.44554D-14
50.	0.27762D-10	0.11379D-10	0.44544D-14
60.	0.27679D-10	0.68503D-11	0.44532D-14
70.	0.27587D-10	0.31909D-11	0.44539D-14
80.	0.27489D-10	0.82185D-12	0.44569D-14
90.	0.27388D-10	0.44211D-14	0.44625D-14
100.	0.27288D-10	0.81578D-12	0.44705D-14
110.	0.27190D-10	0.31445D-11	0.44807D-14
120.	0.27098D-10	0.67051D-11	0.44924D-14
130.	0.27015D-10	0.11071D-10	0.45048D-14
135.	0.26978D-10	0.13394D-10	0.45109D-14
150.	0.26885D-10	0.20092D-10	0.45275D-14
165.	0.26827D-10	0.25006D-10	0.45390D-14
180.	0.26808D-10	0.26808D-10	0.45431D-14

ALPHA = 0.60

THETA	SS	PP	SP
0.	0.31846D-09	0.31846D-09	0.49754D-13
5.	0.31841D-09	0.31591D-09	0.49750D-13
10.	0.31824D-09	0.30835D-09	0.49737D-13
20.	0.31756D-09	0.27940D-09	0.49691D-13
30.	0.31647D-09	0.23550D-09	0.49623D-13
40.	0.31498D-09	0.18245D-09	0.49551D-13
45.	0.31410D-09	0.15459D-09	0.49518D-13
50.	0.31314D-09	0.12700D-09	0.49490D-13
60.	0.31102D-09	0.75927D-10	0.49461D-13
70.	0.30867D-09	0.35123D-10	0.49478D-13
80.	0.30616D-09	0.89882D-11	0.49555D-13
90.	0.30357D-09	0.48636D-13	0.49698D-13
100.	0.30099D-09	0.88327D-11	0.49905D-13
110.	0.29848D-09	0.33933D-10	0.50166D-13
120.	0.29613D-09	0.72206D-10	0.50466D-13
130.	0.29401D-09	0.11910D-09	0.50783D-13
135.	0.29305D-09	0.14406D-09	0.50940D-13
150.	0.29068D-09	0.21616D-09	0.51365D-13
165.	0.28919D-09	0.26920D-09	0.51660D-13
180.	0.28869D-09	0.28869D-09	0.51765D-13

ALPHA = 0.80

THETA	SS	PP	SP
0.	0.17883D-08	0.17883D-08	0.27089D-12
5.	0.17878D-08	0.17734D-08	0.27085D-12
10.	0.17861D-08	0.17293D-08	0.27072D-12
20.	0.17794D-08	0.15610D-08	0.27025D-12
30.	0.17684D-08	0.13078D-08	0.26958D-12
40.	0.17535D-08	0.10051D-08	0.26886D-12
45.	0.17448D-08	0.84770D-09	0.26853D-12
50.	0.17352D-08	0.69303D-09	0.26825D-12
60.	0.17140D-08	0.41007D-09	0.26796D-12
70.	0.16905D-08	0.18772D-09	0.26813D-12
80.	0.16655D-08	0.47567D-10	0.26890D-12
90.	0.16396D-08	0.25972D-12	0.27033D-12
100.	0.16138D-08	0.46013D-10	0.27239D-12
110.	0.15888D-08	0.17583D-09	0.27500D-12
120.	0.15653D-08	0.37291D-09	0.27800D-12
130.	0.15440D-08	0.61405D-09	0.28117D-12
135.	0.15345D-08	0.74256D-09	0.28273D-12
150.	0.15108D-08	0.11146D-08	0.28698D-12
165.	0.14960D-08	0.13896D-08	0.28992D-12
180.	0.14909D-08	0.14909D-08	0.29098D-12

ALPHA = 1.00

THETA	SS	PP	SP
0.	0.68171D-08	0.68171D-08	0.99087D-12
5.	0.68137D-08	0.67575D-08	0.99062D-12
10.	0.68036D-08	0.65812D-08	0.98987D-12
20.	0.67636D-08	0.59114D-08	0.98709D-12
30.	0.66983D-08	0.49130D-08	0.98309D-12
40.	0.66097D-08	0.37356D-08	0.97876D-12
45.	0.65575D-08	0.31313D-08	0.97680D-12
50.	0.65005D-08	0.25429D-08	0.97516D-12
60.	0.63739D-08	0.14832D-08	0.97340D-12
70.	0.62339D-08	0.66891D-09	0.97445D-12
80.	0.60846D-08	0.16706D-09	0.97904D-12
90.	0.59307D-08	0.92433D-12	0.98753D-12
100.	0.57768D-08	0.15780D-09	0.99983D-12
110.	0.56276D-08	0.59802D-09	0.10154D-11
120.	0.54875D-08	0.12617D-08	0.10333D-11
130.	0.53610D-08	0.20721D-08	0.10521D-11
135.	0.53040D-08	0.25046D-08	0.10615D-11
150.	0.51631D-08	0.37616D-08	0.10868D-11
165.	0.50746D-08	0.46977D-08	0.11043D-11
180.	0.50444D-08	0.50444D-08	0.11106D-11

ALPHA = 0.10

THETA	SS	PP	SP
0.	0.26885D-13	0.26885D-13	0.17651D-16
5.	0.26885D-13	0.26681D-13	0.17651D-16
10.	0.26885D-13	0.26074D-13	0.17651D-16
20.	0.26883D-13	0.23738D-13	0.17650D-16
30.	0.26881D-13	0.20161D-13	0.17649D-16
40.	0.26878D-13	0.15774D-13	0.17649D-16
45.	0.26876D-13	0.13441D-13	0.17648D-16
50.	0.26873D-13	0.11108D-13	0.17648D-16
60.	0.26869D-13	0.67261D-14	0.17647D-16
70.	0.26863D-13	0.31556D-14	0.17648D-16
80.	0.26858D-13	0.82629D-15	0.17648D-16
90.	0.26852D-13	0.17639D-16	0.17649D-16
100.	0.26846D-13	0.82595D-15	0.17651D-16
110.	0.26840D-13	0.31529D-14	0.17653D-16
120.	0.26835D-13	0.67177D-14	0.17656D-16
130.	0.26830D-13	0.11090D-13	0.17659D-16
135.	0.26828D-13	0.13417D-13	0.17661D-16
150.	0.26822D-13	0.20117D-13	0.17664D-16
165.	0.26819D-13	0.25022D-13	0.17667D-16
180.	0.26818D-13	0.26818D-13	0.17668D-16

ALPHA = 0.20

THETA	SS	PP	SP
0.	0.17205D-11	0.17205D-11	0.11262D-14
5.	0.17204D-11	0.17073D-11	0.11262D-14
10.	0.17203D-11	0.16683D-11	0.11262D-14
20.	0.17200D-11	0.15183D-11	0.11261D-14
30.	0.17193D-11	0.12887D-11	0.11259D-14
40.	0.17185D-11	0.10075D-11	0.11257D-14
45.	0.17179D-11	0.85807D-12	0.11256D-14
50.	0.17174D-11	0.70883D-12	0.11255D-14
60.	0.17162D-11	0.42878D-12	0.11254D-14
70.	0.17148D-11	0.20098D-12	0.11254D-14
80.	0.17133D-11	0.52580D-13	0.11256D-14
90.	0.17118D-11	0.11233D-14	0.11259D-14
100.	0.17103D-11	0.52494D-13	0.11263D-14
110.	0.17089D-11	0.20029D-12	0.11269D-14
120.	0.17075D-11	0.42663D-12	0.11276D-14
130.	0.17063D-11	0.70424D-12	0.11284D-14
135.	0.17057D-11	0.85197D-12	0.11287D-14
150.	0.17043D-11	0.12774D-11	0.11297D-14
165.	0.17035D-11	0.15891D-11	0.11304D-14
180.	0.17032D-11	0.17032D-11	0.11307D-14

ALPHA = 0.40

THETA	SS	PP	SP
0.	0.11006D-09	0.11006D-09	0.71205D-13
5.	0.11005D-09	0.10921D-09	0.71202D-13
10.	0.11003D-09	0.10667D-09	0.71194D-13
20.	0.10993D-09	0.96922D-10	0.71162D-13
30.	0.10976D-09	0.82060D-10	0.71116D-13
40.	0.10954D-09	0.63949D-10	0.71066D-13
45.	0.10941D-09	0.54368D-10	0.71042D-13
50.	0.10927D-09	0.44826D-10	0.71021D-13
60.	0.10895D-09	0.27011D-10	0.70995D-13
70.	0.10860D-09	0.12612D-10	0.70997D-13
80.	0.10823D-09	0.32878D-11	0.71036D-13
90.	0.10785D-09	0.70455D-13	0.71115D-13
100.	0.10746D-09	0.32657D-11	0.71234D-13
110.	0.10709D-09	0.12436D-10	0.71388D-13
120.	0.10674D-09	0.26460D-10	0.71565D-13
130.	0.10642D-09	0.43653D-10	0.71755D-13
135.	0.10628D-09	0.52804D-10	0.71849D-13
150.	0.10593D-09	0.79186D-10	0.72104D-13
165.	0.10571D-09	0.98538D-10	0.72282D-13
180.	0.10563D-09	0.10563D-09	0.72346D-13

ALPHA = 0.60

THETA	SS	PP	SP
0.	0.12527D-08	0.12527D-08	0.79448D-12
5.	0.12525D-08	0.12427D-08	0.79441D-12
10.	0.12518D-08	0.12130D-08	0.79419D-12
20.	0.12493D-08	0.10993D-08	0.79338D-12
30.	0.12451D-08	0.92684D-09	0.79221D-12
40.	0.12394D-08	0.71836D-09	0.79091D-12
45.	0.12361D-08	0.60886D-09	0.79030D-12
50.	0.12324D-08	0.50038D-09	0.78977D-12
60.	0.12243D-08	0.29948D-09	0.78910D-12
70.	0.12154D-08	0.13889D-09	0.78916D-12
80.	0.12058D-08	0.35981D-10	0.79015D-12
90.	0.11960D-08	0.77527D-12	0.79218D-12
100.	0.11861D-08	0.35415D-10	0.79523D-12
110.	0.11766D-08	0.13440D-09	0.79916D-12
120.	0.11676D-08	0.28535D-09	0.80372D-12
130.	0.11595D-08	0.47030D-09	0.80857D-12
135.	0.11558D-08	0.56879D-09	0.81098D-12
150.	0.11468D-08	0.85317D-09	0.81753D-12
165.	0.11411D-08	0.10624D-08	0.82208D-12
180.	0.11392D-08	0.11392D-08	0.82371D-12

ALPHA = 0.80

THETA	SS	PP	SP
0.	0.70310D-08	0.70310D-08	0.43334D-11
5.	0.70288D-08	0.69726D-08	0.43327D-11
10.	0.70224D-08	0.67996D-08	0.43305D-11
20.	0.69968D-08	0.61593D-08	0.43224D-11
30.	0.69551D-08	0.51457D-08	0.43107D-11
40.	0.68984D-08	0.39571D-08	0.42978D-11
45.	0.68650D-08	0.33390D-08	0.42917D-11
50.	0.68285D-08	0.27311D-08	0.42864D-11
60.	0.67476D-08	0.16182D-08	0.42797D-11
70.	0.66581D-08	0.74287D-09	0.42803D-11
80.	0.65626D-08	0.19062D-09	0.42902D-11
90.	0.64642D-08	0.41415D-11	0.43105D-11
100.	0.63658D-08	0.18496D-09	0.43409D-11
110.	0.62704D-08	0.69802D-09	0.43802D-11
120.	0.61808D-08	0.14771D-08	0.44257D-11
130.	0.60999D-08	0.24306D-08	0.44741D-11
135.	0.60634D-08	0.29388D-08	0.44982D-11
150.	0.59734D-08	0.44097D-08	0.45636D-11
165.	0.59167D-08	0.54969D-08	0.46091D-11
180.	0.58974D-08	0.58974D-08	0.46254D-11

ALPHA = 1.00

THETA	SS	PP	SP
0.	0.26784D-07	0.26784D-07	0.15891D-10
5.	0.26771D-07	0.26551D-07	0.15886D-10
10.	0.26733D-07	0.25861D-07	0.15873D-10
20.	0.26581D-07	0.23238D-07	0.15825D-10
30.	0.26332D-07	0.19325D-07	0.15755D-10
40.	0.25994D-07	0.14707D-07	0.15678D-10
45.	0.25795D-07	0.12335D-07	0.15642D-10
50.	0.25578D-07	0.10024D-07	0.15610D-10
60.	0.25095D-07	0.58569D-08	0.15570D-10
70.	0.24561D-07	0.26499D-08	0.15574D-10
80.	0.23993D-07	0.67048D-09	0.15633D-10
90.	0.23406D-07	0.14747D-10	0.15754D-10
100.	0.22819D-07	0.63676D-09	0.15935D-10
110.	0.22251D-07	0.23826D-08	0.16169D-10
120.	0.21717D-07	0.50160D-08	0.16441D-10
130.	0.21234D-07	0.82331D-08	0.16729D-10
135.	0.21017D-07	0.99496D-08	0.16873D-10
150.	0.20480D-07	0.14939D-07	0.17263D-10
165.	0.20143D-07	0.18653D-07	0.17534D-10
180.	0.20028D-07	0.20028D-07	0.17631D-10

P = 20.00   M = 1.20

ALPHA = 0.10

THETA	SS	PP	SP
0.	0.10435D-12	0.10435D-12	0.27855D-15
5.	0.10435D-12	0.10356D-12	0.27855D-15
10.	0.10435D-12	0.10121D-12	0.27854D-15
20.	0.10434D-12	0.92161D-13	0.27854D-15
30.	0.10433D-12	0.78304D-13	0.27852D-15
40.	0.10432D-12	0.61313D-13	0.27851D-15
45.	0.10431D-12	0.52275D-13	0.27850D-15
50.	0.10431D-12	0.43240D-13	0.27850D-15
60.	0.10429D-12	0.26265D-13	0.27849D-15
70.	0.10427D-12	0.12434D-13	0.27848D-15
80.	0.10425D-12	0.34108D-14	0.27849D-15
90.	0.10423D-12	0.27834D-15	0.27850D-15
100.	0.10421D-12	0.34059D-14	0.27853D-15
110.	0.10419D-12	0.12425D-13	0.27856D-15
120.	0.10417D-12	0.26235D-13	0.27860D-15
130.	0.10415D-12	0.43175D-13	0.27864D-15
135.	0.10414D-12	0.52189D-13	0.27867D-15
150.	0.10412D-12	0.78145D-13	0.27872D-15
165.	0.10411D-12	0.97148D-13	0.27876D-15
180.	0.10410D-12	0.10410D-12	0.27878D-15

ALPHA = 0.20

THETA	SS	PP	SP
0.	0.66770D-11	0.66770D-11	0.17778D-13
5.	0.66769D-11	0.66262D-11	0.17778D-13
10.	0.66765D-11	0.64751D-11	0.17778D-13
20.	0.66751D-11	0.58941D-11	0.17775D-13
30.	0.66728D-11	0.50050D-11	0.17772D-13
40.	0.66697D-11	0.39160D-11	0.17769D-13
45.	0.66678D-11	0.33373D-11	0.17767D-13
50.	0.66658D-11	0.27593D-11	0.17765D-13
60.	0.66613D-11	0.16745D-11	0.17763D-13
70.	0.66563D-11	0.79201D-12	0.17762D-13
80.	0.66510D-11	0.21708D-12	0.17763D-13
90.	0.66456D-11	0.17727D-13	0.17767D-13
100.	0.66401D-11	0.21683D-12	0.17774D-13
110.	0.66348D-11	0.78964D-12	0.17782D-13
120.	0.66298D-11	0.16668D-11	0.17792D-13
130.	0.66254D-11	0.27427D-11	0.17803D-13
135.	0.66233D-11	0.33153D-11	0.17809D-13
150.	0.66183D-11	0.49642D-11	0.17824D-13
165.	0.66152D-11	0.61719D-11	0.17834D-13
180.	0.66141D-11	0.66141D-11	0.17838D-13

ALPHA = 0.40

THETA	SS	PP	SP
0.	0.42697D-09	0.42697D-09	0.11254D-11
5.	0.42694D-09	0.42366D-09	0.11253D-11
10.	0.42685D-09	0.41385D-09	0.11252D-11
20.	0.42648D-09	0.37615D-09	0.11246D-11
30.	0.42589D-09	0.31865D-09	0.11238D-11
40.	0.42509D-09	0.24856D-09	0.11229D-11
45.	0.42461D-09	0.21147D-09	0.11224D-11
50.	0.42409D-09	0.17452D-09	0.11220D-11
60.	0.42294D-09	0.10552D-09	0.11214D-11
70.	0.42167D-09	0.49723D-10	0.11212D-11
80.	0.42032D-09	0.13582D-10	0.11216D-11
90.	0.41892D-09	0.11121D-11	0.11226D-11
100.	0.41752D-09	0.13518D-10	0.11242D-11
110.	0.41616D-09	0.49115D-10	0.11264D-11
120.	0.41489D-09	0.10355D-09	0.11290D-11
130.	0.41374D-09	0.17029D-09	0.11317D-11
135.	0.41322D-09	0.20582D-09	0.11331D-11
150.	0.41194D-09	0.30822D-09	0.11369D-11
165.	0.41114D-09	0.38333D-09	0.11396D-11
180.	0.41087D-09	0.41087D-09	0.11406D-11

ALPHA = 0.60

THETA	SS	PP	SP
0.	0.48566D-08	0.48566D-08	0.12583D-10
5.	0.48558D-08	0.48180D-08	0.12582D-10
10.	0.48535D-08	0.47033D-08	0.12578D-10
20.	0.48442D-08	0.42643D-08	0.12564D-10
30.	0.48290D-08	0.35981D-08	0.12542D-10
40.	0.48083D-08	0.27921D-08	0.12518D-10
45.	0.47962D-08	0.23685D-08	0.12506D-10
50.	0.47829D-08	0.19487D-08	0.12496D-10
60.	0.47534D-08	0.11706D-08	0.12480D-10
70.	0.47208D-08	0.54805D-09	0.12475D-10
80.	0.46861D-08	0.14880D-09	0.12485D-10
90.	0.46503D-08	0.12244D-10	0.12510D-10
100.	0.46144D-08	0.14716D-09	0.12552D-10
110.	0.45797D-08	0.53247D-09	0.12608D-10
120.	0.54471D-08	0.11202D-08	0.12674D-10
130.	0.45176D-08	0.18402D-08	0.12746D-10
135.	0.45043D-08	0.22237D-08	0.12781D-10
150.	0.44715D-08	0.33307D-08	0.12879D-10
165.	0.44509D-08	0.41449D-08	0.12947D-10
180.	0.44439D-08	0.44439D-08	0.12972D-10

ALPHA = 0.80

THETA	SS	PP	SP
0.	0.27234D-07	0.27234D-07	0.68844D-10
5.	0.27226D-07	0.27009D-07	0.68831D-10
10.	0.27203D-07	0.26343D-07	0.68793D-10
20.	0.27110D-07	0.23799D-07	0.68649D-10
30.	0.26958D-07	0.19968D-07	0.68438D-10
40.	0.26752D-07	0.15380D-07	0.68197D-10
45.	0.26630D-07	0.12991D-07	0.68079D-10
50.	0.26498D-07	0.10640D-07	0.67973D-10
60.	0.26203D-07	0.63307D-08	0.67815D-10
70.	0.25878D-07	0.29351D-08	0.67767D-10
80.	0.25531D-07	0.78964D-09	0.67862D-10
90.	0.25173D-07	0.65453D-10	0.68119D-10
100.	0.24815D-07	0.77324D-09	0.68536D-10
110.	0.24468D-07	0.27795D-08	0.69095D-10
120.	0.24142D-07	0.58269D-08	0.69756D-10
130.	0.23848D-07	0.95568D-08	0.70468D-10
135.	0.23715D-07	0.11544D-07	0.70824D-10
150.	0.23387D-07	0.17297D-07	0.71799D-10
165.	0.23181D-07	0.21546D-07	0.72481D-10
180.	0.23111D-07	0.23111D-07	0.72726D-10

ALPHA = 1.00

THETA	SS	PP	SP
0.	0.10363D-06	0.10363D-06	0.25352D-09
5.	0.10358D-06	0.10273D-06	0.25344D-09
10.	0.10344D-06	0.10008D-06	0.25321D-09
20.	0.10288D-06	0.90002D-07	0.25236D-09
30.	0.10198D-06	0.74953D-07	0.25109D-09
40.	0.10075D-06	0.57160D-07	0.24966D-09
45.	0.10003D-06	0.48004D-07	0.24896D-09
50.	0.99237D-07	0.39074D-07	0.24832D-09
60.	0.97482D-07	0.22941D-07	0.24738D-09
70.	0.95541D-07	0.10490D-07	0.24710D-09
80.	0.93473D-07	0.27844D-08	0.24767D-09
90.	0.91339D-07	0.23330D-09	0.24920D-09
100.	0.89205D-07	0.26867D-08	0.25168D-09
110.	0.87137D-07	0.95619D-08	0.25501D-09
120.	0.85196D-07	0.19938D-07	0.25895D-09
130.	0.83441D-07	0.32617D-07	0.26320D-09
135.	0.82651D-07	0.39381D-07	0.26532D-09
150.	0.80698D-07	0.59032D-07	0.27113D-09
165.	0.79471D-07	0.73646D-07	0.27520D-09
180.	0.79052D-07	0.79052D-07	0.27666D-09

P = 20.00

M = 1.30

ALPHA = 0.10

THETA	SS	PP	SP
0.	0.22866D-12	0.22866D-12	0.13829D-14
5.	0.22866D-12	0.22694D-12	0.13829D-14
10.	0.22866D-12	0.22180D-12	0.13829D-14
20.	0.22865D-12	0.20205D-12	0.13828D-14
30.	0.22863D-12	0.17178D-12	0.13827D-14
40.	0.22861D-12	0.13468D-12	0.13827D-14
45.	0.22859D-12	0.11494D-12	0.13826D-14
50.	0.22857D-12	0.95209D-13	0.13826D-14
60.	0.22854D-12	0.58137D-13	0.13825D-14
70.	0.22850D-12	0.27930D-13	0.13825D-14
80.	0.22846D-12	0.82231D-14	0.13825D-14
90.	0.22841D-12	0.13818D-14	0.13826D-14
100.	0.22837D-12	0.82219D-14	0.13827D-14
110.	0.22833D-12	0.27913D-13	0.13828D-14
120.	0.22829D-12	0.58077D-13	0.13830D-14
130.	0.22825D-12	0.95078D-13	0.13832D-14
135.	0.22823D-12	0.11477D-12	0.13833D-14
150.	0.22819D-12	0.17146D-12	0.13836D-14
165.	0.22817D-12	0.21297D-12	0.13838D-14
180.	0.22816D-12	0.22816D-12	0.13839D-14

ALPHA = 0.20

THETA	SS	PP	SP
0.	0.14630D-10	0.14630D-10	0.88285D-13
5.	0.14630D-10	0.14519D-10	0.88284D-13
10.	0.14629D-10	0.14189D-10	0.88281D-13
20.	0.14626D-10	0.12921D-10	0.88269D-13
30.	0.14622D-10	0.10980D-10	0.88251D-13
40.	0.14615D-10	0.86018D-11	0.88231D-13
45.	0.14611D-10	0.73382D-11	0.88221D-13
50.	0.14607D-10	0.60758D-11	0.88211D-13
60.	0.14598D-10	0.37068D-11	0.88196D-13
70.	0.14588D-10	0.17792D-11	0.88189D-13
80.	0.14577D-10	0.52342D-12	0.88193D-13
90.	0.14566D-10	0.88007D-13	0.88209D-13
100.	0.14555D-10	0.52311D-12	0.88236D-13
110.	0.14544D-10	0.17747D-11	0.88275D-13
120.	0.14533D-10	0.36915D-11	0.88322D-13
130.	0.14524D-10	0.60424D-11	0.88373D-13
135.	0.14520D-10	0.72933D-11	0.88398D-13
150.	0.14510D-10	0.10896D-10	0.88469D-13
165.	0.14503D-10	0.13535D-10	0.88518D-13
180.	0.14501D-10	0.14501D-10	0.88536D-13

ALPHA = 0.40

THETA	SS	PP	SP
0.	0.93524D-09	0.93524D-09	0.55942D-11
5.	0.93518D-09	0.92803D-09	0.55939D-11
10.	0.93499D-09	0.90662D-09	0.55931D-11
20.	0.93424D-09	0.82440D-09	0.55901D-11
30.	0.93303D-09	0.69896D-09	0.55856D-11
40.	0.93138D-09	0.54599D-09	0.55803D-11
45.	0.93040D-09	0.46502D-09	0.55777D-11
50.	0.92934D-09	0.38436D-09	0.55753D-11
60.	0.92698D-09	0.23365D-09	0.55715D-11
70.	0.92437D-09	0.11175D-09	0.55697D-11
80.	0.92159D-09	0.32766D-10	0.57706D-11
90.	0.91873D-09	0.55229D-11	0.55746D-11
100.	0.91586D-09	0.32687D-10	0.55818D-11
110.	0.91308D-09	0.11060D-09	0.55917D-11
120.	0.91047D-09	0.22973D-09	0.56036D-11
130.	0.90811D-09	0.37580D-09	0.56167D-11
135.	0.90705D-09	0.45354D-09	0.56232D-11
150.	0.90442D-09	0.67763D-09	0.56412D-11
165.	0.90278D-09	0.84198D-09	0.56539D-11
180.	0.90221D-09	0.90221D-09	0.56585D-11

ALPHA = 0.60

THETA	SS	PP	SP
0.	0.10632D-07	0.10632D-07	0.62657D-10
5.	0.10631D-07	0.10548D-07	0.62650D-10
10.	0.10626D-07	0.10298D-07	0.62629D-10
20.	0.10607D-07	0.93421D-08	0.62552D-10
30.	0.10575D-07	0.78906D-08	0.62436D-10
40.	0.10533D-07	0.61333D-08	0.62302D-10
45.	0.10508D-07	0.52091D-08	0.62236D-10
50.	0.10481D-07	0.42928D-08	0.62174D-10
60.	0.10421D-07	0.25934D-08	0.62075D-10
70.	0.10354D-07	0.12326D-08	0.62029D-10
80.	0.10282D-07	0.35932D-09	0.62053D-10
90.	0.10209D-07	0.60831D-10	0.62156D-10
100.	0.10135D-07	0.35730D-09	0.62339D-10
110.	0.10064D-07	0.12031D-08	0.62593D-10
120.	0.99973D-08	0.24930D-08	0.62899D-10
130.	0.99369D-08	0.40734D-08	0.63233D-10
135.	0.99097D-08	0.49149D-08	0.63401D-10
150.	0.98424D-08	0.73439D-08	0.63863D-10
165.	0.98001D-08	0.91300D-08	0.64188D-10
180.	0.97857D-08	0.97857D-08	0.64305D-10

ALPHA = 0.80

THETA	SS	PP	SP
0.	0.59575D-07	0.59575D-07	0.34368D-09
5.	0.59558D-07	0.59086D-07	0.34361D-09
10.	0.59510D-07	0.57638D-07	0.34340D-09
20.	0.59320D-07	0.52110D-07	0.34262D-09
30.	0.59008D-07	0.43776D-07	0.34147D-09
40.	0.58586D-07	0.33785D-07	0.34013D-09
45.	0.58336D-07	0.28578D-07	0.33947D-09
50.	0.58064D-07	0.23449D-07	0.33885D-09
60.	0.57461D-07	0.14037D-07	0.33787D-09
70.	0.56793D-07	0.66085D-08	0.33740D-09
80.	0.56081D-07	0.19055D-08	0.33764D-09
90.	0.55347D-07	0.32544D-09	0.33867D-09
100.	0.54613D-07	0.18893D-08	0.34050D-09
110.	0.53901D-07	0.63135D-08	0.34303D-09
120.	0.53234D-07	0.13033D-07	0.34610D-09
130.	0.52630D-07	0.21257D-07	0.34943D-09
135.	0.52358D-07	0.25639D-07	0.35111D-09
150.	0.51686D-07	0.38316D-07	0.35573D-09
165.	0.51264D-07	0.47674D-07	0.35897D-09
180.	0.51120D-07	0.51120D-07	0.36014D-09

ALPHA = 1.00

THETA	SS	PP	SP
0.	0.22646D-06	0.22646D-06	0.12700D-08
5.	0.22636D-06	0.22451D-06	0.12695D-08
10.	0.22607D-06	0.21877D-06	0.12683D-08
20.	0.22494D-06	0.19652D-06	0.12637D-08
30.	0.22308D-06	0.16425D-06	0.12568D-08
40.	0.22056D-06	0.12557D-06	0.12488D-08
45.	0.21908D-06	0.10563D-06	0.12449D-08
50.	0.21745D-06	0.86160D-07	0.12412D-08
60.	0.21386D-06	0.50921D-07	0.12353D-08
70.	0.20988D-06	0.23655D-07	0.12326D-08
80.	0.20563D-06	0.67475D-08	0.12340D-08
90.	0.20126D-06	0.11612D-08	0.12401D-08
100.	0.19688D-06	0.66273D-08	0.12510D-08
110.	0.19264D-06	0.21896D-07	0.12661D-08
120.	0.18866D-06	0.44942D-07	0.12844D-08
130.	0.18506D-06	0.73058D-07	0.13043D-08
135.	0.18344D-06	0.88113D-07	0.13143D-08
150.	0.17944D-06	0.13171D-06	0.13418D-08
165.	0.17692D-06	0.16409D-06	0.13611D-08
180.	0.17606D-06	0.17606D-06	0.13681D-08

ALPHA = 0.10

THETA	SS	PP	SP
0.	0.39765D-12	0.39765D-12	0.42682D-14
5.	0.39765D-12	0.39466D-12	0.42682D-14
10.	0.39764D-12	0.38577D-12	0.42682D-14
20.	0.39762D-12	0.35158D-12	0.42680D-14
30.	0.39759D-12	0.29921D-12	0.42678D-14
40.	0.39755D-12	0.23498D-12	0.42675D-14
45.	0.39753D-12	0.20082D-12	0.42674D-14
50.	0.39750D-12	0.16667D-12	0.42673D-14
60.	0.39744D-12	0.10250D-12	0.42671D-14
70.	0.39738D-12	0.50217D-13	0.42669D-14
80.	0.39731D-12	0.16106D-13	0.42669D-14
90.	0.39724D-12	0.42647D-14	0.42671D-14
100.	0.39717D-12	0.16106D-13	0.42674D-14
110.	0.39710D-12	0.50192D-13	0.42678D-14
120.	0.39704D-12	0.10241D-12	0.42684D-14
130.	0.39698D-12	0.16646D-12	0.42689D-14
135.	0.39695D-12	0.20054D-12	0.42692D-14
150.	0.39689D-12	0.29868D-12	0.42701D-14
165.	0.39684D-12	0.37053D-12	0.42706D-14
180.	0.39683D-12	0.39683D-12	0.42708D-14

ALPHA = 0.20

THETA	SS	PP	SP
0.	0.25440D-10	0.25440D-10	0.27255D-12
5.	0.25440D-10	0.25248D-10	0.27255D-12
10.	0.25439D-10	0.24678D-10	0.27253D-12
20.	0.25434D-10	0.22483D-10	0.27250D-12
30.	0.25426D-10	0.19123D-10	0.27244D-12
40.	0.25416D-10	0.15008D-10	0.27237D-12
45.	0.25410D-10	0.12821D-10	0.27234D-12
50.	0.25403D-10	0.10636D-10	0.27230D-12
60.	0.25388D-10	0.65359D-11	0.27225D-12
70.	0.25371D-10	0.31993D-11	0.27222D-12
80.	0.25354D-10	0.10253D-11	0.27222D-12
90.	0.25336D-10	0.27164D-12	0.27226D-12
100.	0.25317D-10	0.10252D-11	0.27234D-12
110.	0.25300D-10	0.31928D-11	0.27245D-12
120.	0.25283D-10	0.65120D-11	0.27258D-12
130.	0.25268D-10	0.10583D-10	0.27273D-12
135.	0.25261D-10	0.12749D-10	0.27281D-12
150.	0.25245D-10	0.18988D-10	0.27302D-12
165.	0.25234D-10	0.23558D-10	0.27317D-12
180.	0.25231D-10	0.25231D-10	0.27322D-12

ALPHA = 0.40

THETA	SS	PP	SP
0.	0.16258D-08	0.16258D-08	0.17285D-10
5.	0.16257D-08	0.16134D-08	0.17284D-10
10.	0.16254D-08	0.15763D-08	0.17281D-10
20.	0.16242D-08	0.14342D-08	0.17271D-10
30.	0.16222D-08	0.12173D-08	0.17257D-10
40.	0.16195D-08	0.95266D-09	0.17239D-10
45.	0.16180D-08	0.81257D-09	0.17230D-10
50.	0.16162D-08	0.67258D-09	0.17222D-10
60.	0.16124D-08	0.41210D-09	0.17208D-10
70.	0.16082D-08	0.20102D-09	0.17201D-10
80.	0.16036D-08	0.64217D-10	0.17201D-10
90.	0.15990D-08	0.17052D-10	0.17211D-10
100.	0.15943D-08	0.64198D-10	0.17231D-10
110.	0.15898D-08	0.19934D-09	0.17259D-10
120.	0.15856D-08	0.40598D-09	0.17294D-10
130.	0.15817D-08	0.65931D-09	0.17332D-10
135.	0.15800D-08	0.79414D-09	0.17352D-10
150.	0.15757D-08	0.11827D-08	0.17405D-10
165.	0.15731D-08	0.14677D-08	0.17443D-10
180.	0.15722D-08	0.15722D-08	0.17457D-10

ALPHA = 0.60

THETA	SS	PP	SP
0.	0.18474D-07	0.18474D-07	0.19388D-09
5.	0.18472D-07	0.18329D-07	0.19386D-09
10.	0.18464D-07	0.17898D-07	0.19379D-09
20.	0.18433D-07	0.16247D-07	0.19354D-09
30.	0.18382D-07	0.13740D-07	0.19316D-09
40.	0.18313D-07	0.10702D-07	0.19271D-09
45.	0.18273D-07	0.91039D-08	0.19248D-09
50.	0.18229D-07	0.75185D-08	0.19227D-09
60.	0.18130D-07	0.45765D-08	0.19192D-09
70.	0.18022D-07	0.22187D-08	0.19172D-09
80.	0.17906D-07	0.70484D-09	0.19173D-09
90.	0.17787D-07	0.18790D-09	0.19199D-09
100.	0.17667D-07	0.70434D-09	0.19250D-09
110.	0.17551D-07	0.21757D-08	0.19322D-09
120.	0.17443D-07	0.44195D-08	0.19411D-09
130.	0.17344D-07	0.71682D-08	0.19510D-09
135.	0.17300D-07	0.86316D-08	0.19559D-09
150.	0.17191D-07	0.12855D-07	0.19696D-09
165.	0.17122D-07	0.15959D-07	0.19793D-09
180.	0.17099D-07	0.17099D-07	0.19828D-09

ALPHA = 0.80

THETA	SS	PP	SP
0.	0.10345D-06	0.10345D-06	0.10658D-08
5.	0.10342D-06	0.10261D-06	0.10655D-08
10.	0.10334D-06	0.10011D-06	0.10649D-08
20.	0.10303D-06	0.90584D-07	0.10623D-08
30.	0.10253D-06	0.76209D-07	0.10585D-08
40.	0.10184D-06	0.58958D-07	0.10540D-08
45.	0.10144D-06	0.49957D-07	0.10518D-08
50.	0.10099D-06	0.41086D-07	0.10496D-08
60.	0.10001D-06	0.24788D-07	0.10461D-08
70.	0.98928D-07	0.11908D-07	0.10441D-08
80.	0.97771D-07	0.37508D-08	0.10443D-08
90.	0.96578D-07	0.10060D-08	0.10469D-08
100.	0.95385D-07	0.37458D-08	0.10519D-08
110.	0.94229D-07	0.11478D-07	0.10592D-08
120.	0.93144D-07	0.23220D-07	0.10681D-08
130.	0.92163D-07	0.37587D-07	0.10779D-08
135.	0.91721D-07	0.45240D-07	0.10828D-08
150.	0.90629D-07	0.67371D-07	0.10965D-08
165.	0.89943D-07	0.83700D-07	0.11062D-08
180.	0.89709D-07	0.89709D-07	0.11097D-08

ALPHA = 1.00

THETA	SS	PP	SP
0.	0.39289D-06	0.39289D-06	0.39497D-08
5.	0.39274D-06	0.38956D-06	0.39484D-08
10.	0.39227D-06	0.37968D-06	0.39444D-08
20.	0.39042D-06	0.34210D-06	0.39291D-08
30.	0.38741D-06	0.28586D-06	0.39064D-08
40.	0.38331D-06	0.21915D-06	0.38797D-08
45.	0.38090D-06	0.18471D-06	0.38663D-08
50.	0.37827D-06	0.15105D-06	0.38536D-08
60.	0.37242D-06	0.90021D-07	0.38325D-08
70.	0.36595D-06	0.42685D-07	0.38208D-08
80.	0.35906D-06	0.13281D-07	0.38217D-08
90.	0.35195D-06	0.35936D-08	0.38371D-08
100.	0.34484D-06	0.13251D-07	0.38672D-08
110.	0.33794D-06	0.40124D-07	0.39104D-08
120.	0.33147D-06	0.80673D-07	0.39634D-08
130.	0.32563D-06	0.13020D-06	0.40218D-08
135.	0.32299D-06	0.15660D-06	0.40514D-08
150.	0.31649D-06	0.23319D-06	0.41331D-08
165.	0.31240D-06	0.29001D-06	0.41907D-08
180.	0.31100D-06	0.31100D-06	0.42115D-08

ALPHA = 0.10

THETA	SS	PP	SP
0.	0.10928D-12	0.10928D-12	0.16262D-16
5.	0.10928D-12	0.10845D-12	0.16262D-16
10.	0.10928D-12	0.10598D-12	0.16261D-16
20.	0.10927D-12	0.96479D-13	0.16261D-16
30.	0.10926D-12	0.81930D-13	0.16261D-16
40.	0.10924D-12	0.64091D-13	0.16260D-16
45.	0.10924D-12	0.54602D-13	0.16260D-16
50.	0.10923D-12	0.45117D-13	0.16260D-16
60.	0.10921D-12	0.27296D-13	0.16259D-16
70.	0.10918D-12	0.12777D-13	0.16260D-16
80.	0.10916D-12	0.33046D-14	0.16260D-16
90.	0.10913D-12	0.16253D-16	0.16262D-16
100.	0.10911D-12	0.33030D-14	0.16264D-16
110.	0.10908D-12	0.12765D-13	0.16266D-16
120.	0.10906D-12	0.27260D-13	0.16269D-16
130.	0.10904D-12	0.45040D-13	0.16272D-16
135.	0.10903D-12	0.54500D-13	0.16273D-16
150.	0.10901D-12	0.81743D-13	0.16277D-16
165.	0.10899D-12	0.10169D-12	0.16280D-16
180.	0.10899D-12	0.10899D-12	0.16281D-16

ALPHA = 0.20

THETA	SS	PP	SP
0.	0.69936D-11	0.69936D-11	0.10375D-14
5.	0.69935D-11	0.69402D-11	0.10375D-14
10.	0.69931D-11	0.67815D-11	0.10375D-14
20.	0.69914D-11	0.61712D-11	0.10374D-14
30.	0.69887D-11	0.52373D-11	0.10373D-14
40.	0.69850D-11	0.40936D-11	0.10371D-14
45.	0.69828D-11	0.34859D-11	0.10371D-14
50.	0.69804D-11	0.28789D-11	0.10370D-14
60.	0.69752D-11	0.17401D-11	0.10370D-14
70.	0.69693D-11	0.81370D-12	0.10371D-14
80.	0.69631D-11	0.21027D-12	0.10373D-14
90.	0.69567D-11	0.10353D-14	0.10376D-14
100.	0.69503D-11	0.20987D-12	0.10381D-14
110.	0.69441D-11	0.81071D-12	0.10387D-14
120.	0.69382D-11	0.17308D-11	0.10394D-14
130.	0.69330D-11	0.28593D-11	0.10402D-14
135.	0.69306D-11	0.34598D-11	0.10405D-14
150.	0.69247D-11	0.51893D-11	0.10415D-14
165.	0.69210D-11	0.64560D-11	0.10422D-14
180.	0.69198D-11	0.69198D-11	0.10424D-14

ALPHA = 0.40

THETA	SS	PP	SP
0.	0.44756D-09	0.44756D-09	0.65581D-13
5.	0.44752D-09	0.44408D-09	0.65578D-13
10.	0.44741D-09	0.43374D-09	0.65572D-13
20.	0.44699D-09	0.39407D-09	0.65548D-13
30.	0.44629D-09	0.33358D-09	0.65513D-13
40.	0.44534D-09	0.25988D-09	0.65478D-13
45.	0.44479D-09	0.22089D-09	0.65462D-13
50.	0.44418D-09	0.18207D-09	0.65450D-13
60.	0.44283D-09	0.10961D-09	0.65441D-13
70.	0.44133D-09	0.51051D-10	0.65459D-13
80.	0.43974D-09	0.13145D-10	0.65512D-13
90.	0.43810D-09	0.64999D-13	0.65602D-13
100.	0.43646D-09	0.13041D-10	0.65729D-13
110.	0.43487D-09	0.50286D-10	0.65887D-13
120.	0.43337D-09	0.10723D-09	0.66066D-13
130.	0.43202D-09	0.17704D-09	0.66254D-13
135.	0.43141D-09	0.21419D-09	0.66346D-13
150.	0.42991D-09	0.32129D-09	0.66597D-13
165.	0.42897D-09	0.39985D-09	0.66770D-13
180.	0.42864D-09	0.42864D-09	0.66831D-13

ALPHA = 0.60

THETA	SS	PP	SP
0.	0.50973D-08	0.50973D-08	0.73141D-12
5.	0.50963D-08	0.50564D-08	0.73135D-12
10.	0.50936D-08	0.49354D-08	0.73119D-12
20.	0.50826D-08	0.44719D-08	0.73057D-12
30.	0.50648D-08	0.37692D-08	0.72969D-12
40.	0.50406D-08	0.29200D-08	0.72877D-12
45.	0.50263D-08	0.24741D-08	0.72837D-12
50.	0.50107D-08	0.20326D-08	0.72806D-12
60.	0.49761D-08	0.12151D-08	0.72782D-12
70.	0.49378D-08	0.56204D-09	0.72830D-12
80.	0.48970D-08	0.14380D-09	0.72965D-12
90.	0.48549D-08	0.71650D-12	0.73197D-12
100.	0.48128D-08	0.14114D-09	0.73522D-12
110.	0.47720D-08	0.54243D-09	0.73926D-12
120.	0.47337D-08	0.11542D-08	0.74385D-12
130.	0.46991D-08	0.19035D-08	0.74866D-12
135.	0.46835D-08	0.23025D-08	0.75104D-12
150.	0.46450D-08	0.34542D-08	0.75745D-12
165.	0.46208D-08	0.43014D-08	0.76188D-12
180.	0.46125D-08	0.46125D-08	0.76346D-12

ALPHA = 0.80

THETA	SS	PP	SP
0.	0.28634D-07	0.28634D-C7	0.39869D-11
5.	0.28625D-07	0.28396D-07	0.39863D-11
10.	0.28598D-07	0.27689D-07	0.39847D-11
20.	0.28488D-07	0.24994D-07	0.39785D-11
30.	0.28310D-07	0.20938D-C7	0.39697D-11
40.	0.28068D-07	0.16091D-07	0.39605D-11
45.	0.27925D-07	0.13571D-07	0.39565D-11
50.	0.27770D-07	0.11095D-07	0.39534D-11
60.	0.27424D-07	0.65644D-08	0.39511D-11
70.	0.27041D-07	0.30048D-C8	0.39558D-11
80.	0.26634D-07	0.76131D-09	0.39693D-11
90.	0.26213D-07	0.38380D-11	0.39925D-11
100.	0.25793D-07	0.73473D-09	0.40249D-11
110.	0.25385D-C7	0.28089D-08	0.40653D-11
120.	0.25003D-07	0.59564D-C8	0.41111D-11
130.	0.24657D-C7	0.98062D-08	0.41592D-11
135.	0.24502D-07	0.11857D-07	0.41829D-11
150.	0.24117D-07	0.17792D-07	0.42470D-11
165.	0.23875D-07	0.22177D-07	0.42913D-11
180.	0.23793D-07	0.23793D-07	0.43071D-11

ALPHA = 1.00

THETA	SS	PP	SP
0.	0.10920D-06	0.10920D-06	0.14607D-10
5.	0.10915D-06	0.10825D-06	0.14604D-10
10.	0.10899D-06	0.10543D-06	0.14594D-10
20.	0.10833D-06	0.94695D-07	0.14557D-10
30.	0.10727D-06	0.78699D-07	0.14505D-10
40.	0.10583D-06	0.59836D-C7	0.14450D-10
45.	0.10498D-06	0.50153D-07	0.14426D-10
50.	0.10405D-06	0.40727D-07	0.14408D-10
60.	0.10199D-06	0.23753D-C7	0.14394D-10
70.	0.99710D-07	0.10711D-07	0.14422D-10
80.	0.97281D-07	0.26753D-C8	0.14503D-10
90.	0.94775D-07	0.13720D-10	0.14641D-10
100.	0.92269D-07	0.25169D-C8	0.14834D-10
110.	0.89840D-07	0.95435D-C8	0.15075D-10
120.	0.87560D-07	0.20129D-07	0.15348D-10
130.	0.85500D-C7	0.33046D-07	0.15634D-10
135.	0.84572D-07	0.39934D-07	0.15776D-10
150.	0.82278D-07	0.59944D-07	0.16158D-10
165.	0.80837D-07	0.74834D-07	0.16421D-10
180.	0.80345D-07	0.80345D-C7	0.16516D-10

ALPHA = 0.10

THETA	SS	PP	SP
0.	0.43000D-12	0.43000D-12	0.25870D-15
5.	0.42999D-12	0.42673D-12	0.25870D-15
10.	0.42999D-12	0.41702D-12	0.25870D-15
20.	0.42996D-12	0.37966D-12	0.25869D-15
30.	0.42992D-12	0.32244D-12	0.25868D-15
40.	0.42987D-12	0.25228D-12	0.25867D-15
45.	0.42984D-12	0.21496D-12	0.25867D-15
50.	0.42980D-12	0.17765D-12	0.25866D-15
60.	0.42972D-12	0.10756D-12	0.25866D-15
70.	0.42963D-12	0.50449D-13	0.25866D-15
80.	0.42954D-12	0.13193D-13	0.25867D-15
90.	0.42945D-12	0.25855D-15	0.25869D-15
100.	0.42935D-12	0.13186D-13	0.25872D-15
110.	0.42926D-12	0.50404D-13	0.25876D-15
120.	0.42917D-12	0.10742D-12	0.25880D-15
130.	0.42909D-12	0.17735D-12	0.25884D-15
135.	0.42906D-12	0.21457D-12	0.25886D-15
150.	0.42897D-12	0.32172D-12	0.25892D-15
165.	0.42891D-12	0.40018D-12	0.25896D-15
180.	0.42889D-12	0.42889D-12	0.25898D-15

ALPHA = 0.20

THETA	SS	PP	SP
0.	0.27519D-10	0.27519D-10	0.16510D-13
5.	0.27518D-10	0.27309D-10	0.16510D-13
10.	0.27517D-10	0.26685D-10	0.16509D-13
20.	0.27510D-10	0.24285D-10	0.16508D-13
30.	0.27500D-10	0.20612D-10	0.16505D-13
40.	0.27486D-10	0.16114D-10	0.16503D-13
45.	0.27477D-10	0.13724D-10	0.16502D-13
50.	0.27468D-10	0.11337D-10	0.16501D-13
60.	0.27448D-10	0.68572D-11	0.16500D-13
70.	0.27426D-10	0.32133D-11	0.16500D-13
80.	0.27402D-10	0.83959D-12	0.16503D-13
90.	0.27378D-10	0.16470D-13	0.16508D-13
100.	0.27353D-10	0.83802D-12	0.16515D-13
110.	0.27329D-10	0.32018D-11	0.16525D-13
120.	0.27307D-10	0.68217D-11	0.16535D-13
130.	0.27287D-10	0.11261D-10	0.16546D-13
135.	0.27278D-10	0.13624D-10	0.16552D-13
150.	0.27255D-10	0.20428D-10	0.16567D-13
165.	0.27241D-10	0.25412D-10	0.16577D-13
180.	0.27237D-10	0.27237D-10	0.16581D-13

ALPHA = 0.40

THETA	SS	PP	SP
0.	0.17610D-08	0.17610D-08	0.10446D-11
5.	0.17608D-08	0.17473D-08	0.10446D-11
10.	0.17604D-08	0.17067D-08	0.10445D-11
20.	0.17588D-08	0.15507D-08	0.10441D-11
30.	0.17561D-08	0.13129D-08	0.10435D-11
40.	0.17525D-08	0.10231D-08	0.10428D-11
45.	0.17504D-08	0.86980D-09	0.10425D-11
50.	0.17480D-08	0.71714D-09	0.10423D-11
60.	0.17429D-08	0.43208D-09	0.10420D-11
70.	0.17372D-08	0.20170D-09	0.10422D-11
80.	0.17311D-08	0.52521D-10	0.10429D-11
90.	0.17248D-08	0.10345D-11	0.10441D-11
100.	0.17185D-08	0.5212CD-10	0.10460D-11
110.	0.17125D-08	0.19877D-09	0.10484D-11
120.	0.17068D-08	0.423C0D-09	0.10511D-11
130.	0.17016D-08	0.69790D-09	0.10540D-11
135.	0.16993D-08	0.84421D-09	0.10554D-11
150.	0.16935D-08	0.12659D-08	0.10592D-11
165.	0.16899D-08	0.15753D-08	0.10619D-11
180.	0.16887D-08	0.16887D-08	0.10628D-11

ALPHA = 0.60

THETA	SS	PP	SP
0.	0.20054D-07	0.20054D-07	0.11672D-10
5.	0.20050D-07	0.19893D-07	0.11671D-10
10.	0.20040D-07	0.19418D-07	0.11668D-10
20.	0.19998D-07	0.17597D-07	0.11657D-10
30.	0.19930D-07	0.14837D-07	0.11641D-10
40.	0.19837D-07	0.11499D-07	0.11624D-10
45.	0.19782D-07	0.97457D-08	0.11617D-10
50.	0.19723D-07	0.80091D-08	0.11610D-10
60.	0.19591D-07	0.47930D-08	0.11604D-10
70.	0.19444D-07	0.22224D-08	0.11608D-10
80.	0.19288D-07	0.57521D-09	0.11626D-10
90.	0.19128D-07	0.11413D-10	0.11659D-10
100.	0.18967D-07	0.56495D-09	0.11707D-10
110.	0.18811D-07	0.21473D-08	0.11767D-10
120.	0.18665D-07	0.456C2D-08	0.11837D-10
130.	0.18532D-07	0.7516CD-08	0.11910D-10
135.	0.18473D-07	0.90897D-08	0.11947D-10
150.	0.18326D-07	0.13633D-07	0.12045D-10
165.	0.18233D-07	0.16974D-07	0.12114D-10
180.	0.18202D-07	0.182C2D-07	0.12138D-10

ALPHA = 0.80

THETA	SS	PP	SP
0.	0.11264D-06	0.11264D-06	0.63788D-10
5.	0.11260D-06	0.11170D-06	0.63778D-10
10.	0.11250D-06	0.10853D-06	0.63749D-10
20.	0.11208D-06	0.98351D-07	0.63641D-10
30.	0.11140D-06	0.82430D-07	0.63485D-10
40.	0.11047D-06	0.63389D-07	0.63317D-10
45.	0.10993D-06	0.53484D-07	0.63241D-10
50.	0.10933D-06	0.43746D-07	0.63178D-10
60.	0.10801D-06	0.25918D-07	0.63109D-10
70.	0.10655D-06	0.11897D-07	0.63150D-10
80.	0.10499D-06	0.30508D-08	0.63329D-10
90.	0.10339D-06	0.61202D-10	0.63660D-10
100.	0.10178D-06	0.29483D-08	0.64138D-10
110.	0.10022D-06	0.11146D-07	0.64744D-10
120.	0.98762D-07	0.23593D-07	0.65439D-10
130.	0.97441D-07	0.38820D-07	0.66172D-10
135.	0.96846D-07	0.46932D-07	0.66536D-10
150.	0.95376D-07	0.70407D-07	0.67520D-10
165.	0.94452D-07	0.87749D-07	0.68203D-10
180.	0.94137D-07	0.94137D-07	0.68447D-10

ALPHA = 1.00

THETA	SS	PP	SP
0.	0.42950D-06	0.42950D-06	0.23455D-09
5.	0.42929D-06	0.42576D-06	0.23449D-09
10.	0.42866D-06	0.41469D-06	0.23432D-09
20.	0.42617D-06	0.37262D-06	0.23367D-09
30.	0.42211D-06	0.30988D-06	0.23275D-09
40.	0.41660D-06	0.23583D-06	0.23175D-09
45.	0.41335D-06	0.19778D-06	0.23129D-09
50.	0.40980D-06	0.16072D-06	0.23091D-09
60.	0.40193D-06	0.93906D-07	0.23050D-09
70.	0.39322D-06	0.42488D-07	0.23075D-09
80.	0.38393D-06	0.10749D-07	0.23182D-09
90.	0.37436D-06	0.21914D-09	0.23379D-09
100.	0.36479D-06	0.10138D-07	0.23664D-09
110.	0.35550D-06	0.38015D-07	0.24025D-09
120.	0.34679D-06	0.80047D-07	0.24439D-09
130.	0.33892D-06	0.13136D-06	0.24876D-09
135.	0.33537D-06	0.15872D-06	0.25093D-09
150.	0.32661D-06	0.23821D-06	0.25680D-09
165.	0.32110D-06	0.29734D-06	0.26086D-09
180.	0.31922D-06	0.31922D-06	0.26232D-09

P = 10.00   M = 1.20

ALPHA = 0.10

THETA	SS	PP	SP
0.	0.16668D-11	0.16668D-11	0.40671D-14
5.	0.16668D-11	0.16542D-11	0.40671D-14
10.	0.16668D-11	0.16166D-11	0.40670D-14
20.	0.16667D-11	0.14721D-11	0.40669D-14
30.	0.16666D-11	0.12507D-11	0.40667D-14
40.	0.16664D-11	0.97921D-12	0.40666D-14
45.	0.16662D-11	0.83482D-12	0.40665D-14
50.	0.16661D-11	0.69046D-12	0.40664D-14
60.	0.16658D-11	0.41925D-12	0.40663D-14
70.	0.16655D-11	0.19828D-12	0.40663D-14
80.	0.16652D-11	0.54113D-13	0.40664D-14
90.	0.16648D-11	0.40643D-14	0.40666D-14
100.	0.16645D-11	0.54093D-13	0.40670D-14
110.	0.16641D-11	0.19812D-12	0.40675D-14
120.	0.16638D-11	0.41875D-12	0.40681D-14
130.	0.16635D-11	0.68939D-12	0.40688D-14
135.	0.16634D-11	0.83339D-12	0.40691D-14
150.	0.16631D-11	0.12481D-11	0.40699D-14
165.	0.16629D-11	0.15517D-11	0.40705D-14
180.	0.16628D-11	0.16628D-11	0.40708D-14

ALPHA = 0.20

THETA	SS	PP	SP
0.	0.10667D-09	0.10667D-09	0.25967D-12
5.	0.10667D-09	0.10586D-09	0.25967D-12
10.	0.10666D-09	0.10344D-09	0.25966D-12
20.	0.10664D-09	0.94161D-10	0.25963D-12
30.	0.10660D-09	0.79952D-10	0.25959D-12
40.	0.10655D-09	0.62551D-10	0.25954D-12
45.	0.10652D-09	0.53304D-10	0.25952D-12
50.	0.10649D-09	0.44067D-10	0.25950D-12
60.	0.10641D-09	0.26733D-10	0.25947D-12
70.	0.10633D-09	0.12632D-10	0.25947D-12
80.	0.10624D-09	0.34448D-11	0.25949D-12
90.	0.10616D-09	0.25897D-12	0.25956D-12
100.	0.10607D-09	0.34395D-11	0.25966D-12
110.	0.10598D-09	0.12591D-10	0.25979D-12
120.	0.10590D-09	0.26605D-10	0.25994D-12
130.	0.10582D-09	0.43793D-10	0.26011D-12
135.	0.10579D-09	0.52940D-10	0.26019D-12
150.	0.10571D-09	0.79282D-10	0.26041D-12
165.	0.10566D-09	0.98575D-10	0.26057D-12
180.	0.10564D-09	0.10564D-09	0.26062D-12

ALPHA = 0.40

THETA	SS	PP	SP
0.	0.68256D-08	0.68256D-08	0.16461D-10
5.	0.68250D-08	0.67727D-08	0.16460D-10
10.	0.68235D-08	0.66157D-08	0.16458D-10
20.	0.68176D-08	0.60129D-08	0.16451D-10
30.	0.68079D-08	0.50936D-08	0.16440D-10
40.	0.67947D-08	0.39728D-08	0.16427D-10
45.	0.67869D-08	0.33797D-08	0.16421D-10
50.	0.67784D-08	0.27890D-08	0.16416D-10
60.	0.67595D-08	0.16857D-08	0.16408D-10
70.	0.67387D-08	0.79360D-09	0.16408D-10
80.	0.67164D-08	0.21575D-09	0.16415D-10
90.	0.66935D-08	0.16280D-10	0.16431D-10
100.	0.66706D-08	0.21439D-09	0.16457D-10
110.	0.66483D-08	0.78307D-09	0.16490D-10
120.	0.66275D-08	0.16527D-08	0.16530D-10
130.	0.66086D-08	0.27189D-08	0.16572D-10
135.	0.66001D-08	0.32864D-08	0.16592D-10
150.	0.65791D-08	0.49220D-08	0.16649D-10
165.	0.65659D-08	0.61217D-08	0.16689D-10
180.	0.65614D-08	0.65614D-08	0.16703D-10

ALPHA = 0.60

THETA	SS	PP	SP
0.	0.77720D-07	0.77720D-07	0.18450D-09
5.	0.77708D-07	0.77102D-07	0.18448D-09
10.	0.77669D-07	0.75267D-07	0.18443D-09
20.	0.77516D-07	0.68238D-07	0.18424D-09
30.	0.77267D-07	0.57575D-07	0.18395D-09
40.	0.76929D-07	0.44674D-07	0.18363D-09
45.	0.76729D-07	0.37894D-07	0.18348D-09
50.	0.76511D-07	0.31174D-07	0.18334D-09
60.	0.76028D-07	0.18721D-07	0.18315D-09
70.	0.75493D-07	0.87580D-08	0.18313D-09
80.	0.74924D-07	0.23679D-08	0.18332D-09
90.	0.74336D-07	0.17987D-09	0.18374D-09
100.	0.73748D-07	0.23330D-08	0.18439D-09
110.	0.73178D-07	0.84882D-08	0.18525D-09
120.	0.72643D-07	0.17876D-07	0.18626D-09
130.	0.72160D-07	0.29378D-07	0.18733D-09
135.	0.71942D-07	0.35502D-07	0.18787D-09
150.	0.71405D-07	0.53179D-07	0.18933D-09
165.	0.71066D-07	0.66178D-07	0.19034D-09
180.	0.70951D-07	0.70951D-07	0.19071D-09

ALPHA = 0.80

THETA	SS	PP	SP
0.	0.43647D-06	0.43647D-06	0.10130D-08
5.	0.43635D-06	0.43287D-06	0.10129D-08
10.	0.43596D-06	0.42219D-06	0.10124D-08
20.	0.43443D-06	0.38142D-06	0.10104D-08
30.	0.43194D-06	0.32000D-06	0.10075D-08
40.	0.42856D-06	0.24646D-06	0.10043D-08
45.	0.42657D-06	0.20817D-06	0.10028D-08
50.	0.42440D-06	0.17049D-06	0.10014D-08
60.	0.41957D-06	0.10142D-06	0.99957D-09
70.	0.41423D-06	0.46993D-07	0.99933D-09
80.	0.40854D-06	0.12559D-07	0.10012D-08
90.	0.40266D-06	0.96678D-09	0.10054D-08
100.	0.39679D-06	0.12251D-07	0.10120D-08
110.	0.39110D-06	0.44258D-07	0.10205D-08
120.	0.38576D-06	0.92976D-07	0.10306D-08
130.	0.38093D-06	0.15254D-06	0.10413D-08
135.	0.37876D-06	0.18427D-06	0.10467D-08
150.	0.37339D-06	0.27609D-06	0.10612D-08
165.	0.37001D-06	0.34389D-06	0.10714D-08
180.	0.36886D-06	0.36886D-06	0.10750D-08

ALPHA = 1.00

THETA	SS	PP	SP
0.	0.16640D-05	0.16640D-05	0.37487D-08
5.	0.16632D-05	0.16496D-05	0.37476D-08
10.	0.16609D-05	0.16070D-05	0.37446D-08
20.	0.16518D-05	0.14452D-05	0.37329D-08
30.	0.16370D-05	0.12036D-05	0.37159D-08
40.	0.16168D-05	0.91786D-06	0.36968D-08
45.	0.16050D-05	0.77084D-06	0.36877D-08
50.	0.15920D-05	0.62744D-06	0.36796D-08
60.	0.15632D-05	0.36836D-06	0.36684D-08
70.	0.15314D-05	0.16840D-06	0.36669D-08
80.	0.14975D-05	0.44604D-07	0.36781D-08
90.	0.14625D-05	0.34729D-08	0.37032D-08
100.	0.14275D-05	0.42529D-07	0.37422D-08
110.	0.13935D-05	0.15234D-06	0.37933D-08
120.	0.13617D-05	0.31806D-06	0.38532D-08
130.	0.13329D-05	0.52048D-06	0.39171D-08
135.	0.13200D-05	0.62842D-06	0.39490D-08
150.	0.12879D-05	0.94184D-06	0.40359D-08
165.	0.12678D-05	0.11748D-05	0.40965D-08
180.	0.12609D-05	0.12609D-05	0.41183D-08

ALPHA = 0.10

THETA	SS	PP	SP
0.	0.36446D-11	0.36446D-11	0.20100D-13
5.	0.36446D-11	0.36171D-11	0.20100D-13
10.	0.36446D-11	0.35352D-11	0.20100D-13
20.	0.36444D-11	0.32201D-11	0.20099D-13
30.	0.36441D-11	0.27376D-11	0.20098D-13
40.	0.36437D-11	0.21458D-11	0.20097D-13
45.	0.36434D-11	0.18310D-11	0.20097D-13
50.	0.36431D-11	0.15164D-11	0.20096D-13
60.	0.36426D-11	0.92517D-12	0.20095D-13
70.	0.36419D-11	0.44346D-12	0.20095D-13
80.	0.36412D-11	0.12919D-12	0.20095D-13
90.	0.36405D-11	0.20085D-13	0.20096D-13
100.	0.36398D-11	0.12915D-12	0.20098D-13
110.	0.36391D-11	0.44315D-12	0.20100D-13
120.	0.36384D-11	0.92415D-12	0.20103D-13
130.	0.36378D-11	0.15142D-11	0.20106D-13
135.	0.36375D-11	0.18281D-11	0.20108D-13
150.	0.36369D-11	0.27322D-11	0.20112D-13
165.	0.36365D-11	0.33940D-11	0.20115D-13
180.	0.36363D-11	0.36363D-11	0.20116D-13

ALPHA = 0.20

THETA	SS	PP	SP
0.	0.23324D-09	0.23324D-09	0.12839D-11
5.	0.23324D-09	0.23147D-09	0.12839D-11
10.	0.23323D-09	0.22621D-09	0.12838D-11
20.	0.23318D-09	0.20598D-09	0.12836D-11
30.	0.23310D-09	0.17501D-09	0.12834D-11
40.	0.23300D-09	0.13708D-09	0.12831D-11
45.	0.23293D-09	0.11693D-09	0.12830D-11
50.	0.23286D-09	0.96791D-10	0.12829D-11
60.	0.23271D-09	0.59003D-10	0.12827D-11
70.	0.23254D-09	0.28258D-10	0.12826D-11
80.	0.23237D-09	0.82264D-11	0.12827D-11
90.	0.23218D-09	0.12800D-11	0.12830D-11
100.	0.23200D-09	0.82173D-11	0.12834D-11
110.	0.23182D-09	0.28177D-10	0.12840D-11
120.	0.23165D-09	0.58742D-10	0.12847D-11
130.	0.23150D-09	0.96231D-10	0.12855D-11
135.	0.23143D-09	0.11618D-09	0.12858D-11
150.	0.23126D-09	0.17363D-09	0.12869D-11
165.	0.23115D-09	0.21571D-09	0.12876D-11
180.	0.23112D-09	0.23112D-09	0.12879D-11

P = 10.00

M = 1.30

ALPHA = 0.40

THETA	SS	PP	SP
0.	0.14925D-07	0.14925D-07	0.81520D-10
5.	0.14924D-07	0.14809D-07	0.81516D-10
10.	0.14920D-07	0.14468D-07	0.81505D-10
20.	0.14908D-07	0.13155D-07	0.81463D-10
30.	0.14888D-07	0.11152D-07	0.81402D-10
40.	0.14861D-07	0.87095D-08	0.81332D-10
45.	0.14845D-07	0.74168D-08	0.81297D-10
50.	0.14827D-07	0.61290D-08	0.81266D-10
60.	0.14788D-07	0.37229D-08	0.81217D-10
70.	0.14745D-07	0.17768D-08	0.81199D-10
80.	0.14700D-07	0.51579D-09	0.81221D-10
90.	0.14652D-07	0.80542D-10	0.81288D-10
100.	0.14605D-07	0.51348D-09	0.81399D-10
110.	0.14559D-07	0.17560D-08	0.81551D-10
120.	0.14516D-07	0.36561D-08	0.81731D-10
130.	0.14477D-07	0.59856D-08	0.81926D-10
135.	0.14460D-07	0.72255D-08	0.82024D-10
150.	0.14417D-07	0.10759D-07	0.82292D-10
165.	0.14390D-07	0.13420D-07	0.82480D-10
180.	0.14380D-07	0.14380D-07	0.82547D-10

ALPHA = 0.60

THETA	SS	PP	SP
0.	0.16994D-06	0.16994D-06	0.91627D-09
5.	0.16991D-06	0.16860D-06	0.91617D-09
10.	0.16984D-06	0.16460D-06	0.91589D-09
20.	0.16952D-06	0.14931D-06	0.91482D-09
30.	0.16901D-06	0.12610D-06	0.91325D-09
40.	0.16831D-06	0.97957D-07	0.91145D-09
45.	0.16790D-06	0.83219D-07	0.91057D-09
50.	0.16745D-06	0.68567D-07	0.90975D-09
60.	0.16645D-06	0.41395D-07	0.90852D-09
70.	0.16535D-06	0.19637D-07	0.90805D-09
80.	0.16418D-06	0.56722D-08	0.90861D-09
90.	0.16297D-06	0.89121D-09	0.91032D-09
100.	0.16176D-06	0.56128D-08	0.91318D-09
110.	0.16058D-06	0.19104D-07	0.91706D-09
120.	0.15948D-06	0.39682D-07	0.92168D-09
130.	0.15848D-06	0.64893D-07	0.92668D-09
135.	0.15803D-06	0.78316D-07	0.92918D-09
150.	0.15693D-06	0.11706D-06	0.93605D-09
165.	0.15623D-06	0.14554D-06	0.94087D-09
180.	0.15599D-06	0.15599D-06	0.94260D-09

41

ALPHA = 0.80

THETA	SS	PP	SP
0.	0.95438D-06	0.95438D-06	0.50515D-08
5.	0.95412D-06	0.94655D-06	0.50505D-08
10.	0.95332D-06	0.92335D-06	0.50477D-08
20.	0.95018D-06	0.83475D-06	0.50371D-08
30.	0.94505D-06	0.70120D-06	0.50214D-08
40.	0.93808D-06	0.54109D-06	0.50034D-08
45.	0.93398D-06	0.45764D-06	0.49945D-08
50.	0.92949D-06	0.37546D-06	0.49864D-08
60.	0.91955D-06	0.22463D-06	0.49741D-08
70.	0.90854D-06	0.10560D-06	0.49694D-08
80.	0.89681D-06	0.30273D-07	0.49750D-08
90.	0.88471D-06	0.48012D-08	0.49921D-08
100.	0.87262D-06	0.29680D-07	0.50207D-08
110.	0.86088D-06	0.10027D-06	0.50594D-08
120.	0.84988D-06	0.20752D-06	0.51056D-08
130.	0.83993D-06	0.33876D-06	0.51555D-08
135.	0.83545D-06	0.40867D-06	0.51805D-08
150.	0.82438D-06	0.61087D-06	0.52491D-08
165.	0.81742D-06	0.76011D-06	0.52972D-08
180.	0.81504D-06	0.81504D-06	0.53145D-08

ALPHA = 1.00

THETA	SS	PP	SP
0.	0.36384D-05	0.36384D-05	0.18796D-07
5.	0.36368D-05	0.36072D-05	0.18790D-07
10.	0.36321D-05	0.35149D-05	0.18773D-07
20.	0.36134D-05	0.31639D-05	0.18710D-07
30.	0.35828D-05	0.26390D-05	0.18616D-07
40.	0.35413D-05	0.20174D-05	0.18509D-07
45.	0.35168D-05	0.16970D-05	0.18456D-07
50.	0.34901D-05	0.13842D-05	0.18408D-07
60.	0.34308D-05	0.81790D-06	0.18334D-07
70.	0.33652D-05	0.37963D-06	0.18307D-07
80.	0.32953D-05	0.10765D-06	0.18340D-07
90.	0.32232D-05	0.17304D-07	0.18441D-07
100.	0.31511D-05	0.10411D-06	0.18612D-07
110.	0.30811D-05	0.34786D-06	0.18843D-07
120.	0.30155D-05	0.71589D-06	0.19118D-07
130.	0.29562D-05	0.11654D-05	0.19415D-07
135.	0.29295D-05	0.14051D-05	0.19565D-07
150.	0.28635D-05	0.21006D-05	0.19974D-07
165.	0.28221D-05	0.26170D-05	0.20260D-07
180.	0.28079D-05	0.28079D-05	0.20363D-07

ALPHA = 0.10

THETA	SS	PP	SP
0.	0.63187D-11	0.63187D-11	0.61714D-13
5.	0.63186D-11	0.62711D-11	0.61713D-13
10.	0.63185D-11	0.61297D-11	0.61713D-13
20.	0.63182D-11	0.55859D-11	0.61711D-13
30.	0.63177D-11	0.47529D-11	0.61708D-13
40.	0.63171D-11	0.37314D-11	0.61704D-13
45.	0.63167D-11	0.31880D-11	0.61702D-13
50.	0.63162D-11	0.26448D-11	0.61700D-13
60.	0.63153D-11	0.16242D-11	0.61698D-13
70.	0.63142D-11	0.79258D-12	0.61696D-13
80.	0.63130D-11	0.25002D-12	0.61697D-13
90.	0.63119D-11	0.61665D-13	0.61699D-13
100.	0.63107D-11	0.24998D-12	0.61704D-13
110.	0.63096D-11	0.79209D-12	0.61711D-13
120.	0.63085D-11	0.16226D-11	0.61719D-13
130.	0.63075D-11	0.26412D-11	0.61727D-13
135.	0.63071D-11	0.31833D-11	0.61732D-13
150.	0.63060D-11	0.47441D-11	0.61744D-13
165.	0.63053D-11	0.58868D-11	0.61752D-13
180.	0.63051D-11	0.63051D-11	0.61755D-13

ALPHA = 0.20

THETA	SS	PP	SP
0.	0.40438D-09	0.40438D-09	0.39434D-11
5.	0.40437D-09	0.40132D-09	0.39433D-11
10.	0.40435D-09	0.39224D-09	0.39432D-11
20.	0.40427D-09	0.35732D-09	0.39426D-11
30.	0.40415D-09	0.30387D-09	0.39418D-11
40.	0.40397D-09	0.23840D-09	0.39409D-11
45.	0.40387D-09	0.20360D-09	0.39405D-11
50.	0.40376D-09	0.16884D-09	0.39400D-11
60.	0.40351D-09	0.10360D-09	0.39393D-11
70.	0.40324D-09	0.50514D-10	0.39390D-11
80.	0.40294D-09	0.15925D-10	0.39391D-11
90.	0.40264D-09	0.39308D-11	0.39398D-11
100.	0.40234D-09	0.15914D-10	0.39410D-11
110.	0.40205D-09	0.50389D-10	0.39426D-11
120.	0.40178D-09	0.10318D-09	0.39447D-11
130.	0.40153D-09	0.16794D-09	0.39469D-11
135.	0.40142D-09	0.20239D-09	0.39480D-11
150.	0.40114D-09	0.30163D-09	0.39511D-11
165.	0.40097D-09	0.37430D-09	0.39533D-11
180.	0.40091D-09	0.40091D-09	0.39541D-11

ALPHA = 0.40

THETA	SS	PP	SP
0.	0.25877D-07	0.25877D-07	0.25076D-09
5.	0.25875D-07	0.25678D-07	0.25075D-09
10.	0.25870D-07	0.25088D-07	0.25071D-09
20.	0.25850D-07	0.22823D-07	0.25057D-09
30.	0.25817D-07	0.19368D-07	0.25037D-09
40.	0.25773D-07	0.15152D-07	0.25013D-09
45.	0.25746D-07	0.12921D-07	0.25002D-09
50.	0.25718D-07	0.10697D-07	0.24991D-09
60.	0.25654D-07	0.65413D-08	0.24973D-09
70.	0.25584D-07	0.31789D-08	0.24964D-09
80.	0.25509D-07	0.99961D-09	0.24967D-09
90.	0.25432D-07	0.24755D-09	0.24984D-09
100.	0.25355D-07	0.99693D-09	0.25015D-09
110.	0.25280D-07	0.31469D-08	0.25058D-09
120.	0.25210D-07	0.64346D-08	0.25110D-09
130.	0.25147D-07	0.10465D-07	0.25167D-09
135.	0.25118D-07	0.12611D-07	0.25195D-09
150.	0.25047D-07	0.18793D-07	0.25274D-09
165.	0.25003D-07	0.23327D-07	0.25330D-09
180.	0.24988D-07	0.24988D-07	0.25350D-09

ALPHA = 0.60

THETA	SS	PP	SP
0.	0.29468D-06	0.29468D-06	0.28257D-08
5.	0.29464D-06	0.29236D-06	0.28253D-08
10.	0.29451D-06	0.28548D-06	0.28244D-08
20.	0.29399D-06	0.25912D-06	0.28209D-08
30.	0.29315D-06	0.21909D-06	0.28157D-08
40.	0.29201D-06	0.17060D-06	0.28096D-08
45.	0.29134D-06	0.14509D-06	0.28066D-08
50.	0.29061D-06	0.11978D-06	0.28038D-08
60.	0.28899D-06	0.72819D-07	0.27992D-08
70.	0.28719D-06	0.35184D-07	0.27970D-08
80.	0.28527D-06	0.11014D-07	0.27978D-08
90.	0.28329D-06	0.27434D-08	0.28021D-08
100.	0.28131D-06	0.10946D-07	0.28100D-08
110.	0.27940D-06	0.34364D-07	0.28210D-08
120.	0.27760D-06	0.70084D-07	0.28343D-08
130.	0.27597D-06	0.11384D-06	0.28489D-08
135.	0.27524D-06	0.13714D-06	0.28563D-08
150.	0.27343D-06	0.20436D-06	0.28765D-08
165.	0.27229D-06	0.25377D-06	0.28907D-08
180.	0.27190D-06	0.27190D-06	0.28959D-08

ALPHA = 0.80

THETA	SS	PP	SP
0.	0.16551D-05	0.16551D-C5	0.15635D-07
5.	0.16547D-05	0.16417D-05	0.15632D-07
10.	0.16534D-05	0.16017D-05	0.15623D-07
20.	0.16483D-05	0.14492D-C5	0.15588D-07
30.	0.16399D-05	0.12190D-05	0.15536D-07
40.	0.16285D-05	0.94285D-06	0.15475D-07
45.	0.16218D-05	0.79876D-06	0.15445D-07
50.	0.16145D-05	0.65675D-06	0.15417D-07
60.	0.15983D-05	0.39584D-06	0.15371D-07
70.	0.15803D-05	0.18963D-06	0.15349D-07
80.	0.15611D-05	0.58963D-07	0.15357D-07
90.	0.15414D-05	0.14814D-07	0.15400D-07
100.	0.15216D-05	0.58277D-07	0.15478D-07
110.	0.15025D-05	0.18143D-C6	0.15588D-07
120.	0.14845D-05	0.36853D-C6	0.15722D-07
130.	0.14683D-05	0.59746D-C6	0.15867D-07
135.	0.14610D-05	0.71939D-06	0.15941D-07
150.	0.14429D-05	0.10719D-05	0.16143D-07
165.	0.14315D-05	0.13320D-C5	0.16285D-07
180.	0.14277D-05	0.14277D-05	0.16337D-07

ALPHA = 1.00

THETA	SS	PP	SP
0.	0.63111D-05	0.63111D-05	0.58461D-07
5.	0.63086D-05	0.62576D-C5	0.58443D-07
10.	0.63008D-05	0.60989D-05	0.58388D-07
20.	0.62702D-05	0.54952D-C5	0.58179D-07
30.	0.62203D-05	0.45916D-C5	0.57868D-07
40.	0.61525D-05	0.35197D-05	0.57507D-07
45.	0.61126D-05	0.29665D-05	0.57327D-07
50.	0.60690D-05	0.24256D-C5	0.57158D-07
60.	0.59721D-05	0.14448D-C5	0.56886D-07
70.	0.58650D-05	0.68381D-06	0.56752D-07
80.	0.57509D-05	0.21059D-06	0.56801D-07
90.	0.56332D-05	0.53565D-07	0.57058D-07
100.	0.55154D-C5	0.20650D-06	0.57526D-07
110.	0.54013D-05	0.63496D-06	0.58182D-07
120.	0.52942D-05	0.12820D-05	0.58976D-07
130.	0.51974D-05	0.20722D-05	0.59845D-07
135.	0.51537D-05	0.24934D-05	0.60283D-07
150.	0.50460D-05	0.37148D-C5	0.61488D-07
165.	0.49783D-05	0.46206D-05	0.62336D-07
180.	0.49552D-05	0.49552D-C5	0.62641D-07

P = 5.00   M = 1.05

ALPHA = 0.10

THETA	SS	PP	SP
0.	0.17481D-11	0.17481D-11	0.20370D-15
5.	0.17481D-11	0.17348D-11	0.20370D-15
10.	0.17480D-11	0.16953D-11	0.20370D-15
20.	0.17479D-11	0.15433D-11	0.20370D-15
30.	0.17477D-11	0.13106D-11	0.20370D-15
40.	0.17475D-11	0.10252D-11	0.20369D-15
45.	0.17473D-11	0.87342D-12	0.20369D-15
50.	0.17472D-11	0.72167D-12	0.20369D-15
60.	0.17468D-11	0.43659D-12	0.20370D-15
70.	0.17465D-11	0.20433D-12	0.20370D-15
80.	0.17460D-11	0.52807D-13	0.20372D-15
90.	0.17456D-11	0.20363D-15	0.20374D-15
100.	0.17452D-11	0.52776D-13	0.20377D-15
110.	0.17448D-11	0.20412D-12	0.20381D-15
120.	0.17444D-11	0.43597D-12	0.20385D-15
130.	0.17440D-11	0.72035D-12	0.20389D-15
135.	0.17439D-11	0.87166D-12	0.20390D-15
150.	0.17435D-11	0.13074D-11	0.20396D-15
165.	0.17432D-11	0.16264D-11	0.20399D-15
180.	0.17431D-11	0.17431D-11	0.20400D-15

ALPHA = 0.20

THETA	SS	PP	SP
0.	0.11189D-09	0.11189D-09	0.12999D-13
5.	0.11189D-09	0.11103D-09	0.12999D-13
10.	0.11188D-09	0.10849D-09	0.12998D-13
20.	0.11185D-09	0.98729D-10	0.12998D-13
30.	0.11180D-09	0.83786D-10	0.12997D-13
40.	0.11174D-09	0.65488D-10	0.12996D-13
45.	0.11170D-09	0.55766D-10	0.12996D-13
50.	0.11166D-09	0.46054D-10	0.12995D-13
60.	0.11157D-09	0.27834D-10	0.12996D-13
70.	0.11147D-09	0.13014D-10	0.12999D-13
80.	0.11137D-09	0.33604D-11	0.13003D-13
90.	0.11126D-09	0.12980D-13	0.13008D-13
100.	0.11115D-09	0.33525D-11	0.13016D-13
110.	0.11104D-09	0.12961D-10	0.13025D-13
120.	0.11094D-09	0.27674D-10	0.13035D-13
130.	0.11085D-09	0.45717D-10	0.13045D-13
135.	0.11081D-09	0.55317D-10	0.13050D-13
150.	0.11071D-09	0.82966D-10	0.13063D-13
165.	0.11065D-09	0.10321D-09	0.13072D-13
180.	0.11063D-09	0.11063D-09	0.13075D-13

ALPHA = 0.40

THETA	SS	PP	SP
0.	0.71636D-08	0.71636D-08	0.82206D-12
5.	0.71630D-08	0.71079D-08	0.82204D-12
10.	0.71611D-08	0.69425D-08	0.82198D-12
20.	0.71539D-08	0.63073D-08	0.82179D-12
30.	0.71420D-08	0.53389D-08	0.82154D-12
40.	0.71258D-08	0.41590D-08	0.82132D-12
45.	0.71163D-08	0.35350D-08	0.82127D-12
50.	0.71060D-08	0.29136D-08	0.82126D-12
60.	0.70829D-08	0.17537D-08	0.82147D-12
70.	0.70574D-08	0.81668D-09	0.82204D-12
80.	0.70303D-08	0.21014D-09	0.82306D-12
90.	0.70023D-08	0.81721D-12	0.82454D-12
100.	0.69742D-08	0.20812D-09	0.82647D-12
110.	0.69471D-08	0.80318D-09	0.82876D-12
120.	0.69216D-08	0.17127D-08	0.83128D-12
130.	0.68985D-08	0.28272D-08	0.83388D-12
135.	0.68882D-08	0.34202D-08	0.83515D-12
150.	0.68625D-08	0.51289D-08	0.83854D-12
165.	0.68464D-08	0.63818D-08	0.84086D-12
180.	0.68409D-08	0.68409D-08	0.84169D-12

ALPHA = 0.60

THETA	SS	PP	SP
0.	0.81651D-07	0.81651D-07	0.91766D-11
5.	0.81635D-07	0.80997D-07	0.91762D-11
10.	0.81588D-07	0.79057D-07	0.91748D-11
20.	0.81402D-07	0.71629D-07	0.91698D-11
30.	0.81097D-07	0.60370D-07	0.91634D-11
40.	0.80683D-07	0.46763D-07	0.91579D-11
45.	0.80440D-07	0.39619D-07	0.91564D-11
50.	0.80174D-07	0.32545D-07	0.91562D-11
60.	0.79583D-07	0.19451D-07	0.91615D-11
70.	0.78930D-07	0.89949D-08	0.91763D-11
80.	0.78234D-07	0.23002D-08	0.92023D-11
90.	0.77516D-07	0.90525D-11	0.92403D-11
100.	0.76798D-07	0.22485D-08	0.92897D-11
110.	0.76102D-07	0.86489D-08	0.93484D-11
120.	0.75448D-07	0.18399D-07	0.94131D-11
130.	0.74858D-07	0.30330D-07	0.94797D-11
135.	0.74592D-07	0.36678D-07	0.95122D-11
150.	0.73935D-07	0.54988D-07	0.95991D-11
165.	0.73522D-07	0.68442D-07	0.96586D-11
180.	0.73381D-07	0.73381D-07	0.96798D-11

ALPHA = 0.80

THETA	SS	PP	SP
0.	0.45919D-06	0.45919D-06	0.50089D-10
5.	0.45903D-06	0.45536D-06	0.50084D-10
10.	0.45856D-06	0.44402D-06	0.50070D-10
20.	0.45669D-06	0.40077D-06	0.50021D-10
30.	0.45365D-06	0.33571D-06	0.49956D-10
40.	0.44952D-06	0.25794D-06	0.49901D-10
45.	0.44709D-06	0.21752D-06	0.49886D-10
50.	0.44443D-06	0.17780D-06	0.49885D-10
60.	0.43853D-06	0.10516D-06	0.49938D-10
70.	0.43201D-06	0.48120D-07	0.50085D-10
80.	0.42506D-06	0.12189D-07	0.50345D-10
90.	0.41788D-06	0.48848D-10	0.50725D-10
100.	0.41071D-06	0.11672D-07	0.51218D-10
110.	0.40376D-06	0.44664D-07	0.51804D-10
120.	0.39723D-06	0.94650D-07	0.52451D-10
130.	0.39133D-06	0.15568D-06	0.53116D-10
135.	0.38868D-06	0.18814D-06	0.53440D-10
150.	0.38211D-06	0.28194D-06	0.54309D-10
165.	0.37799D-06	0.35112D-06	0.54903D-10
180.	0.37658D-06	0.37658D-06	0.55114D-10

ALPHA = 1.00

THETA	SS	PP	SP
0.	0.17537D-05	0.17537D-05	0.18386D-09
5.	0.17528D-05	0.17384D-05	0.18383D-09
10.	0.17500D-05	0.16930D-05	0.18375D-09
20.	0.17389D-05	0.15205D-05	0.18345D-09
30.	0.17207D-05	0.12635D-05	0.18307D-09
40.	0.16961D-05	0.96040D-06	0.18274D-09
45.	0.16816D-05	0.80485D-06	0.18265D-09
50.	0.16658D-05	0.65346D-06	0.18264D-09
60.	0.16306D-05	0.38092D-06	0.18295D-09
70.	0.15917D-05	0.17170D-06	0.18383D-09
80.	0.15503D-05	0.42892D-07	0.18538D-09
90.	0.15075D-05	0.17646D-09	0.18765D-09
100.	0.14648D-05	0.39811D-07	0.19059D-09
110.	0.14233D-05	0.15110D-06	0.19408D-09
120.	0.13844D-05	0.31826D-06	0.19793D-09
130.	0.13493D-05	0.52157D-06	0.20190D-09
135.	0.13334D-05	0.62972D-06	0.20383D-09
150.	0.12943D-05	0.94304D-06	0.20901D-09
165.	0.12697D-05	0.11754D-05	0.21255D-09
180.	0.12613D-05	0.12613D-05	0.21381D-09

ALPHA = 0.10

THETA	SS	PP	SP
0.	0.68735D-11	0.68735D-11	
5.	0.68734D-11	0.68212D-11	0.32272D-14
10.	0.68733D-11	0.66660D-11	0.32272D-14
20.	0.68729D-11	0.60687D-11	0.32272D-14
30.	0.68722D-11	0.51539D-11	0.32271D-14
			0.32271D-14
40.	0.68712D-11	0.40322D-11	0.32270D-14
45.	0.68707D-11	0.34356D-11	0.32270D-14
50.	0.68701D-11	0.28391D-11	0.32269D-14
60.	0.68687D-11	0.17186D-11	0.32270D-14
70.	0.68672D-11	0.80561D-12	0.32271D-14
80.	0.68656D-11	0.21001D-12	0.32273D-14
90.	0.68640D-11	0.32258D-14	0.32276D-14
100.	0.68623D-11	0.20987D-12	0.32280D-14
110.	0.68607D-11	0.80479D-12	0.32286D-14
120.	0.68592D-11	0.17161D-11	0.32292D-14
130.	0.68579D-11	0.28340D-11	0.32298D-14
135.	0.68573D-11	0.34288D-11	0.32300D-14
150.	0.68558D-11	0.51416D-11	0.32308D-14
165.	0.68548D-11	0.63955D-11	0.32314D-14
180.	0.68545D-11	0.68545D-11	0.32316D-14

ALPHA = 0.20

THETA	SS	PP	SP
0.	0.43999D-09	0.43999D-09	
5.	0.43998D-09	0.43663D-09	0.20603D-12
10.	0.43995D-09	0.42665D-09	0.20603D-12
20.	0.43984D-09	0.38827D-09	0.20603D-12
30.	0.43966D-09	0.32954D-09	0.20601D-12
			0.20599D-12
40.	0.43942D-09	0.25761D-09	0.20598D-12
45.	0.43928D-09	0.21939D-09	0.20597D-12
50.	0.43912D-09	0.18122D-09	0.20597D-12
60.	0.43878D-09	0.10959D-09	0.20597D-12
70.	0.43839D-09	0.51323D-10	0.20600D-12
80.	0.43799D-09	0.13369D-10	0.20605D-12
90.	0.43756D-09	0.20568D-12	0.20614D-12
100.	0.43714D-09	0.13334D-10	0.20625D-12
110.	0.43673D-09	0.51113D-10	0.20638D-12
120.	0.43635D-09	0.10896D-09	0.20653D-12
130.	0.43601D-09	0.17951D-09	0.20669D-12
135.	0.43585D-09	0.21766D-09	0.20676D-12
150.	0.43546D-09	0.32637D-09	0.20696D-12
165.	0.43522D-09	0.40599D-09	0.20710D-12
180.	0.43514D-09	0.43514D-09	0.20715D-12

ALPHA = 0.40

THETA	SS	PP	SP
0.	0.28182D-07	0.28182D-07	0.13056D-10
5.	0.28180D-07	0.27963D-07	0.13056D-10
10.	0.28172D-07	0.27313D-07	0.13055D-10
20.	0.28144D-07	0.24816D-07	0.13051D-10
30.	0.28099D-07	0.21010D-07	0.13046D-10
40.	0.28037D-07	0.16371D-07	0.13041D-10
45.	0.28000D-07	0.13917D-07	0.13040D-10
50.	0.27960D-07	0.11473D-07	0.13039D-10
60.	0.27871D-07	0.69110D-08	0.13040D-10
70.	0.27773D-07	0.32243D-08	0.13048D-10
80.	0.27669D-07	0.83727D-09	0.13062D-10
90.	0.27561D-07	0.12967D-10	0.13083D-10
100.	0.27453D-07	0.82842D-09	0.13111D-10
110.	0.27349D-07	0.317C4D-08	0.13146D-10
120.	0.27251D-07	0.675C6D-08	0.13184D-10
130.	0.27162D-07	0.11138D-C7	0.13223D-10
135.	0.27122D-07	0.13473D-07	0.13242D-10
150.	0.27023D-07	0.202C0D-07	0.13294D-10
165.	0.26961D-07	0.25133D-07	0.13330D-10
180.	0.26940D-07	0.2694CD-07	0.13342D-10

ALPHA = 0.60

THETA	SS	PP	SP
0.	0.32144D-06	0.32144D-06	0.14624D-09
5.	0.32138D-06	0.31887D-06	0.14623D-09
10.	0.32120D-06	0.31124D-06	0.14621D-09
20.	0.32048D-06	0.282C5D-06	0.14612D-09
30.	0.31931D-06	0.23778D-06	0.14599D-09
40.	0.31772D-06	0.18426D-06	0.14587D-09
45.	0.31678D-06	0.15616D-06	0.14583D-09
50.	0.31575D-06	0.12832D-06	0.14581D-09
60.	0.31348D-06	0.76771D-07	0.14585D-09
70.	0.31097D-06	0.35580D-07	0.14603D-09
80.	0.30829D-06	0.91850D-C8	0.14639D-09
90.	0.30553D-06	0.14396D-09	0.14694D-09
100.	0.30276D-06	0.89623D-08	0.14766D-09
110.	0.30009D-06	0.34199D-07	0.14854D-09
120.	0.29757D-06	0.72660D-C7	0.14952D-09
130.	0.29530D-06	0.11973D-06	0.15053D-09
135.	0.29428D-06	0.14478D-06	0.15102D-09
150.	0.29175D-06	0.217C3D-06	0.15235D-09
165.	0.29016D-06	0.27013D-06	0.15326D-09
180.	0.28962D-06	0.28962D-06	0.15358D-09

ALPHA = 0.80

THETA	SS	PP	SP
0.	0.18094D-05	0.18094D-05	0.80224D-09
5.	0.18088D-05	0.17944D-05	0.80215D-09
10.	0.18070D-05	0.17498D-05	0.80190D-09
20.	0.17998D-05	0.15758D-05	0.80097D-09
30.	0.17881D-05	0.13240D-05	0.79972D-09
40.	0.17722D-05	0.10180D-05	0.79854D-09
45.	0.17629D-05	0.85883D-06	0.79812D-09
50.	0.17526D-05	0.70237D-06	0.79789D-09
60.	0.17300D-05	0.41602D-06	0.79828D-09
70.	0.17048D-05	0.19089D-06	0.80012D-09
80.	0.16781D-05	0.48892D-07	0.80371D-09
90.	0.16505D-05	0.77945D-09	0.80918D-09
100.	0.16229D-05	0.46628D-07	0.81644D-09
110.	0.15961D-05	0.17710D-06	0.82519D-09
120.	0.15710D-05	0.37495D-06	0.83494D-09
130.	0.15483D-05	0.61660D-06	0.84503D-09
135.	0.15381D-05	0.74519D-06	0.84997D-09
150.	0.15129D-05	0.11167D-05	0.86322D-09
165.	0.14970D-05	0.13907D-05	0.87233D-09
180.	0.14916D-05	0.14916D-05	0.87557D-09

ALPHA = 1.00

THETA	SS	PP	SP
0.	0.69189D-05	0.69189D-05	0.29649D-08
5.	0.69153D-05	0.68586D-05	0.29644D-08
10.	0.69045D-05	0.66803D-05	0.29629D-08
20.	0.68618D-05	0.60024D-05	0.29574D-08
30.	0.67920D-05	0.49914D-05	0.29499D-08
40.	0.66973D-05	0.37981D-05	0.29429D-08
45.	0.66415D-05	0.31851D-05	0.29403D-08
50.	0.65805D-05	0.25880D-05	0.29390D-08
60.	0.64453D-05	0.15118D-05	0.29413D-08
70.	0.62956D-05	0.68396D-06	0.29523D-08
80.	0.61361D-05	0.17308D-06	0.29737D-08
90.	0.59716D-05	0.28291D-08	0.30063D-08
100.	0.58071D-05	0.15959D-06	0.30496D-08
110.	0.56476D-05	0.60175D-06	0.31017D-08
120.	0.54980D-05	0.12670D-05	0.31598D-08
130.	0.53627D-05	0.20768D-05	0.32200D-08
135.	0.53018D-05	0.25077D-05	0.32494D-08
150.	0.51512D-05	0.37562D-05	0.33284D-08
165.	0.50566D-05	0.46822D-05	0.33827D-08
180.	0.50243D-05	0.50243D-05	0.34020D-08

P = 5.00   M = 1.20

ALPHA = 0.10

THETA	SS	PP	SP
0.	0.26563D-10	0.26563D-10	0.50247D-13
5.	0.26563D-10	0.26362D-10	0.50247D-13
10.	0.26563D-10	0.25763D-10	0.50247D-13
20.	0.26561D-10	0.23458D-10	0.50246D-13
30.	0.26559D-10	0.19928D-10	0.50244D-13
40.	0.26555D-10	0.15599D-10	0.50243D-13
45.	0.26553D-10	0.13297D-10	0.50242D-13
50.	0.26551D-10	0.10995D-10	0.50242D-13
60.	0.26546D-10	0.66705D-11	0.50241D-13
70.	0.26540D-10	0.31470D-11	0.50242D-13
80.	0.26534D-10	0.84832D-12	0.50245D-13
90.	0.26528D-10	0.50221D-13	0.50249D-13
100.	0.26522D-10	0.84772D-12	0.50255D-13
110.	0.26516D-10	0.31438D-11	0.50262D-13
120.	0.26511D-10	0.66612D-11	0.50270D-13
130.	0.26506D-10	0.10976D-10	0.50279D-13
135.	0.26503D-10	0.13271D-10	0.50283D-13
150.	0.26498D-10	0.19882D-10	0.50295D-13
165.	0.26494D-10	0.24722D-10	0.50303D-13
180.	0.26493D-10	0.26493D-10	0.50306D-13

ALPHA = 0.20

THETA	SS	PP	SP
0.	0.17008D-08	0.17008D-08	0.32109D-11
5.	0.17007D-08	0.16878D-08	0.32108D-11
10.	0.17006D-08	0.16493D-08	0.32108D-11
20.	0.17002D-08	0.15012D-08	0.32105D-11
30.	0.16996D-08	0.12745D-08	0.32101D-11
40.	0.16987D-08	0.99691D-09	0.32097D-11
45.	0.16981D-08	0.84940D-09	0.32095D-11
50.	0.16976D-08	0.70204D-09	0.32094D-11
60.	0.16963D-08	0.42554D-09	0.32093D-11
70.	0.16949D-08	0.20059D-09	0.32096D-11
80.	0.16933D-08	0.54041D-10	0.32102D-11
90.	0.16918D-08	0.32042D-11	0.32113D-11
100.	0.16902D-08	0.53889D-10	0.32128D-11
110.	0.16887D-08	0.19977D-09	0.32147D-11
120.	0.16873D-08	0.42316D-09	0.32168D-11
130.	0.16860D-08	0.69714D-09	0.32190D-11
135.	0.16854D-08	0.84292D-09	0.32201D-11
150.	0.16840D-08	0.12628D-08	0.32230D-11
165.	0.16831D-08	0.15702D-08	0.32251D-11
180.	0.16828D-08	0.16828D-08	0.32258D-11

ALPHA = 0.40

THETA	SS	PP	SP
0.	0.10903D-06	0.10903D-06	0.20423D-09
5.	0.10902D-06	0.10819D-06	0.20422D-09
10.	0.10900D-06	0.10568D-06	0.20420D-09
20.	0.10889D-06	0.96043D-07	0.20413D-09
30.	0.10872D-06	0.81347D-07	0.20403D-09
40.	0.10849D-06	0.63433D-07	0.20393D-09
45.	0.10836D-06	0.53955D-07	0.20388D-09
50.	0.10821D-06	0.44514D-07	0.20385D-09
60.	0.10788D-06	0.26883D-07	0.20383D-09
70.	0.10752D-06	0.12628D-07	0.20389D-09
80.	0.10713D-06	0.33944D-08	0.20405D-09
90.	0.10673D-06	0.20252D-09	0.20433D-09
100.	0.10633D-06	0.33552D-08	0.20472D-09
110.	0.10594D-06	0.12417D-07	0.20520D-09
120.	0.10558D-06	0.26274D-07	0.20574D-09
130.	0.10525D-06	0.43258D-07	0.20631D-09
135.	0.10510D-06	0.52296D-07	0.20659D-09
150.	0.10474D-06	0.78339D-07	0.20734D-09
165.	0.10451D-06	0.97433D-07	0.20786D-09
180.	0.10443D-06	0.10443D-06	0.20805D-09

ALPHA = 0.60

THETA	SS	PP	SP
0.	0.12454D-05	0.12454D-05	0.23022D-08
5.	0.12452D-05	0.12355D-05	0.23020D-08
10.	0.12445D-05	0.12061D-05	0.23015D-08
20.	0.12419D-05	0.10934D-05	0.22997D-08
30.	0.12375D-05	0.92238D-06	0.22972D-08
40.	0.12316D-05	0.71555D-06	0.22945D-08
45.	0.12281D-05	0.60685D-06	0.22934D-08
50.	0.12244D-05	0.49914D-06	0.22925D-08
60.	0.12159D-05	0.29954D-06	0.22920D-08
70.	0.12066D-05	0.13987D-06	0.22935D-08
80.	0.11967D-05	0.37443D-07	0.22978D-08
90.	0.11864D-05	0.22586D-08	0.23049D-08
100.	0.11762D-05	0.36440D-07	0.23148D-08
110.	0.11663D-05	0.13446D-06	0.23271D-08
120.	0.11570D-05	0.28394D-06	0.23410D-08
130.	0.11485D-05	0.46695D-06	0.23555D-08
135.	0.11447D-05	0.56434D-06	0.23627D-08
150.	0.11354D-05	0.84528D-06	0.23820D-08
165.	0.11295D-05	0.10517D-05	0.23954D-08
180.	0.11275D-05	0.11275D-05	0.24002D-08

ALPHA = 0.80

THETA	SS	PP	SP
0.	0.70249D-05	0.70249D-05	0.12746D-07
5.	0.70227D-05	0.69669D-05	0.12744D-07
10.	0.70160D-05	0.67949D-05	0.12739D-07
20.	0.69894D-05	0.61383D-05	0.12721D-07
30.	0.69460D-05	0.51494D-05	0.12696D-07
40.	0.68871D-05	0.39654D-05	0.12669D-07
45.	0.68524D-05	0.33489D-05	0.12658D-07
50.	0.68145D-05	0.27423D-05	0.12649D-07
60.	0.67304D-05	0.16305D-05	0.12644D-07
70.	0.66373D-05	0.75460D-06	0.12659D-07
80.	0.65381D-05	0.20078D-06	0.12702D-07
90.	0.64358D-05	0.12310D-07	0.12773D-07
100.	0.63335D-05	0.19076D-06	0.12872D-07
110.	0.62343D-05	0.70055D-06	0.12994D-07
120.	0.61413D-05	0.14747D-05	0.13133D-07
130.	0.60572D-05	0.24207D-05	0.13278D-07
135.	0.60193D-05	0.29243D-05	0.13350D-07
150.	0.59257D-05	0.43792D-05	0.13543D-07
165.	0.58668D-05	0.54520D-05	0.13677D-07
180.	0.58467D-05	0.58467D-05	0.13725D-07

ALPHA = 1.00

THETA	SS	PP	SP
0.	0.26932D-04	0.26932D-04	0.47692D-07
5.	0.26919D-04	0.26699D-04	0.47682D-07
10.	0.26879D-04	0.26010D-04	0.47653D-07
20.	0.26720D-04	0.23352D-04	0.47546D-07
30.	0.26461D-04	0.19481D-04	0.47394D-07
40.	0.26110D-04	0.14857D-04	0.47235D-07
45.	0.25903D-04	0.12477D-04	0.47168D-07
50.	0.25678D-04	0.10156D-04	0.47116D-07
60.	0.25176D-04	0.59624D-05	0.47083D-07
70.	0.24622D-04	0.27251D-05	0.47177D-07
80.	0.24030D-04	0.71882D-06	0.47428D-07
90.	0.23421D-04	0.45094D-07	0.47852D-07
100.	0.22811D-04	0.65910D-06	0.48442D-07
110.	0.22220D-04	0.24030D-05	0.49172D-07
120.	0.21665D-04	0.50335D-05	0.50000D-07
130.	0.21164D-04	0.82394D-05	0.50866D-07
135.	0.20938D-04	0.99460D-05	0.51294D-07
150.	0.20380D-04	0.14890D-04	0.52447D-07
165.	0.20029D-04	0.18556D-04	0.53243D-07
180.	0.19909D-04	0.19909D-04	0.53527D-07

ALPHA = 0.10

THETA	SS	PP	SP
0.	0.57785D-10	0.57785D-10	0.24552D-12
5.	0.57785D-10	0.57348D-10	0.24552D-12
10.	0.57784D-10	0.56048D-10	0.24552D-12
20.	0.57781D-10	0.51046D-10	0.24551D-12
30.	0.57776D-10	0.43385D-10	0.24550D-12
40.	0.57768D-10	0.33991D-10	0.24549D-12
45.	0.57764D-10	0.28994D-10	0.24549D-12
50.	0.57759D-10	0.23999D-10	0.24549D-12
60.	0.57749D-10	0.14614D-10	0.24548D-12
70.	0.57737D-10	0.69667D-11	0.24548D-12
80.	0.57725D-10	0.19776D-11	0.24549D-12
90.	0.57712D-10	0.24537D-12	0.24551D-12
100.	0.57699D-10	0.19762D-11	0.24553D-12
110.	0.57687D-10	0.69597D-11	0.24557D-12
120.	0.57675D-10	0.14594D-10	0.24560D-12
130.	0.57665D-10	0.23959D-10	0.24564D-12
135.	0.57660D-10	0.28941D-10	0.24566D-12
150.	0.57649D-10	0.43289D-10	0.24572D-12
165.	0.57641D-10	0.53794D-10	0.24575D-12
180.	0.57639D-10	0.57639D-10	0.24577D-12

ALPHA = 0.20

THETA	SS	PP	SP
0.	0.37007D-08	0.37007D-08	0.15703D-10
5.	0.37006D-08	0.36726D-08	0.15702D-10
10.	0.37004D-08	0.35890D-08	0.15702D-10
20.	0.36996D-08	0.32675D-08	0.15700D-10
30.	0.36982D-08	0.27756D-08	0.15698D-10
40.	0.36963D-08	0.21730D-08	0.15696D-10
45.	0.36952D-08	0.18528D-08	0.15695D-10
50.	0.36940D-08	0.15330D-08	0.15694D-10
60.	0.36913D-08	0.93268D-09	0.15693D-10
70.	0.36883D-08	0.44429D-09	0.15693D-10
80.	0.36852D-08	0.12607D-09	0.15695D-10
90.	0.36819D-08	0.15665D-10	0.15700D-10
100.	0.36787D-08	0.12571D-09	0.15706D-10
110.	0.36755D-08	0.44249D-09	0.15715D-10
120.	0.36725D-08	0.92762D-09	0.15724D-10
130.	0.36698D-08	0.15226D-08	0.15734D-10
135.	0.36686D-08	0.18392D-08	0.15739D-10
150.	0.36657D-08	0.27510D-08	0.15753D-10
165.	0.36638D-08	0.34187D-08	0.15763D-10
180.	0.36631D-08	0.36631D-08	0.15766D-10

P = 5.00   M = 1.30

ALPHA = 0.40

THETA	SS	PP	SP
0.	0.23747D-06	0.23747D-06	0.10022D-08
5.	0.23745D-06	0.23563D-06	0.10022D-08
10.	0.23740D-06	0.23019D-06	0.10021D-08
20.	0.23718D-06	0.20927D-06	0.10017D-08
30.	0.23682D-06	0.17736D-06	0.10011D-08
40.	0.23634D-06	0.13845D-06	0.10005D-08
45.	0.23606D-06	0.11786D-06	0.10002D-08
50.	0.23575D-06	0.97347D-07	0.99995D-09
60.	0.23506D-06	0.59024D-07	0.99967D-09
70.	0.23430D-06	0.28029D-07	0.99977D-09
80.	0.23350D-06	0.79412D-08	0.10004D-08
90.	0.23266D-06	0.99269D-09	0.10015D-08
100.	0.23183D-06	0.78492D-08	0.10032D-08
110.	0.23102D-06	0.27569D-07	0.10053D-08
120.	0.23026D-06	0.57729D-07	0.10078D-08
130.	0.22957D-06	0.94659D-07	0.10104D-08
135.	0.22926D-06	0.11437D-06	0.10117D-08
150.	0.22850D-06	0.17106D-06	0.10152D-08
165.	0.22802D-06	0.21262D-06	0.10176D-08
180.	0.22785D-06	0.22785D-06	0.10185D-08

ALPHA = 0.60

THETA	SS	PP	SP
0.	0.27167D-05	0.27167D-05	0.11364D-07
5.	0.27163D-05	0.26952D-05	0.11363D-07
10.	0.27149D-05	0.26313D-05	0.11360D-07
20.	0.27093D-05	0.23865D-05	0.11350D-07
30.	0.27002D-05	0.20150D-05	0.11335D-07
40.	0.26879D-05	0.15653D-05	0.11319D-07
45.	0.26807D-05	0.13288D-05	0.11312D-07
50.	0.26727D-05	0.10944D-05	0.11306D-07
60.	0.26551D-05	0.65965D-06	0.11298D-07
70.	0.26357D-05	0.31156D-06	0.11301D-07
80.	0.26149D-05	0.88037D-07	0.11317D-07
90.	0.25935D-05	0.11120D-07	0.11346D-07
100.	0.25721D-05	0.85680D-07	0.11389D-07
110.	0.25514D-05	0.29979D-06	0.11443D-07
120.	0.25319D-05	0.62647D-06	0.11506D-07
130.	0.25143D-05	0.10265D-05	0.11573D-07
135.	0.25064D-05	0.12394D-05	0.11606D-07
150.	0.24868D-05	0.18535D-05	0.11696D-07
165.	0.24745D-05	0.23047D-05	0.11758D-07
180.	0.24703D-05	0.24703D-05	0.11780D-07

ALPHA = 0.80

THETA	SS	PP	SP
0.	0.15358D-04	0.15358D-04	0.63442D-07
5.	0.15353D-04	0.15231D-04	0.63433D-07
10.	0.15339D-04	0.14858D-04	0.63406D-07
20.	0.15283D-04	0.13431D-04	0.63303D-07
30.	0.15193D-04	0.11280D-04	0.63156D-07
40.	0.15070D-04	0.87020D-05	0.62995D-07
45.	0.14997D-04	0.73583D-05	0.62921D-07
50.	0.14918D-04	0.60350D-05	0.62858D-07
60.	0.14742D-04	0.36067D-05	0.62786D-07
70.	0.14548D-04	0.16900D-05	0.62814D-07
80.	0.14340D-04	0.47562D-06	0.62967D-07
90.	0.14127D-04	0.61000D-07	0.63260D-07
100.	0.13913D-04	0.45208D-06	0.63689D-07
110.	0.13706D-04	0.15724D-05	0.64235D-07
120.	0.13511D-04	0.32753D-05	0.64863D-07
130.	0.13335D-04	0.53573D-05	0.65529D-07
135.	0.13256D-04	0.64655D-05	0.65859D-07
150.	0.13061D-04	0.96674D-05	0.66754D-07
165.	0.12938D-04	0.12028D-04	0.67375D-07
180.	0.12896D-04	0.12896D-04	0.67597D-07

ALPHA = 1.00

THETA	SS	PP	SP
0.	0.59041D-04	0.59041D-04	0.24001D-06
5.	0.59013D-04	0.58535D-04	0.23995D-06
10.	0.58930D-04	0.57038D-04	0.23979D-06
20.	0.58599D-04	0.51343D-04	0.23918D-06
30.	0.58058D-04	0.42828D-04	0.23830D-06
40.	0.57324D-04	0.32741D-04	0.23734D-06
45.	0.56892D-04	0.27541D-04	0.23690D-06
50.	0.56420D-04	0.22463D-04	0.23653D-06
60.	0.55373D-04	0.13270D-04	0.23610D-06
70.	0.54213D-04	0.61498D-05	0.23626D-06
80.	0.52978D-04	0.17211D-05	0.23718D-06
90.	0.51704D-04	0.22545D-06	0.23892D-06
100.	0.50430D-04	0.15807D-05	0.24148D-06
110.	0.49195D-04	0.54489D-05	0.24473D-06
120.	0.48036D-04	0.11294D-04	0.24848D-06
130.	0.46988D-04	0.18424D-04	0.25245D-06
135.	0.46516D-04	0.22220D-04	0.25441D-06
150.	0.45350D-04	0.33215D-04	0.25975D-06
165.	0.44617D-04	0.41360D-04	0.26345D-06
180.	0.44367D-04	0.44367D-04	0.26478D-06

P = 5.00   M = 1.40

ALPHA = 0.10

THETA	SS	PP	SP
0.	0.99463D-10	0.99463D-10	0.74412D-12
5.	0.99463D-10	0.98712D-10	0.74412D-12
10.	0.99461D-10	0.96483D-10	0.74411D-12
20.	0.99456D-10	0.87902D-10	0.74409D-12
30.	0.99447D-10	0.74758D-10	0.74406D-12
40.	0.99435D-10	0.58642D-10	0.74403D-12
45.	0.99428D-10	0.50069D-10	0.74401D-12
50.	0.99420D-10	0.41498D-10	0.74400D-12
60.	0.99402D-10	0.25396D-10	0.74398D-12
70.	0.99383D-10	0.12276D-10	0.74397D-12
80.	0.99363D-10	0.37159D-11	0.74399D-12
90.	0.99342D-10	0.74363D-12	0.74404D-12
100.	0.99321D-10	0.37134D-11	0.74411D-12
110.	0.99300D-10	0.12264D-10	0.74420D-12
120.	0.99281D-10	0.25363D-10	0.74431D-12
130.	0.99264D-10	0.41431D-10	0.74442D-12
135.	0.99256D-10	0.49981D-10	0.74448D-12
150.	0.99236D-10	0.74599D-10	0.74463D-12
165.	0.99224D-10	0.92623D-10	0.74474D-12
180.	0.99220D-10	0.99220D-10	0.74478D-12

ALPHA = 0.20

THETA	SS	PP	SP
0.	0.63715D-08	0.63715D-08	0.47630D-10
5.	0.63713D-08	0.63232D-08	0.47629D-10
10.	0.63710D-08	0.61798D-08	0.47628D-10
20.	0.63696D-08	0.56283D-08	0.47623D-10
30.	0.63673D-08	0.47841D-08	0.47615D-10
40.	0.63642D-08	0.37502D-08	0.47607D-10
45.	0.63624D-08	0.32007D-08	0.47602D-10
50.	0.63604D-08	0.26518D-08	0.47599D-10
60.	0.63559D-08	0.16215D-08	0.47594D-10
70.	0.63510D-08	0.78328D-09	0.47593D-10
80.	0.63458D-08	0.23705D-09	0.47598D-10
90.	0.63404D-08	0.47505D-10	0.47610D-10
100.	0.63350D-08	0.23640D-09	0.47628D-10
110.	0.63297D-08	0.78021D-09	0.47651D-10
120.	0.63248D-08	0.16131D-08	0.47678D-10
130.	0.63204D-08	0.26345D-08	0.47707D-10
135.	0.63184D-08	0.31780D-08	0.47722D-10
150.	0.63134D-08	0.47433D-08	0.47761D-10
165.	0.63103D-08	0.58896D-08	0.47789D-10
180.	0.63093D-08	0.63093D-08	0.47799D-10

ALPHA = 0.40

THETA	SS	PP	SP
0.	0.40926D-06	0.40926D-06	0.30500D-08
5.	0.40923D-06	0.40612D-06	0.30498D-08
10.	0.40914D-06	0.39677D-06	0.30495D-08
20.	0.40878D-06	0.36086D-06	0.30481D-08
30.	0.40820D-06	0.30608D-06	0.30462D-08
40.	0.40740D-06	0.23927D-06	0.30440D-08
45.	0.40693D-06	0.20390D-06	0.30429D-08
50.	0.40642D-06	0.16866D-06	0.30420D-08
60.	0.40528D-06	0.10280D-06	0.30407D-08
70.	0.40403D-06	0.49519D-07	0.30406D-08
80.	0.40269D-06	0.14974D-07	0.30419D-08
90.	0.40130D-06	0.30181D-08	0.30448D-08
100.	0.39992D-06	0.14808D-07	0.30494D-08
110.	0.39858D-06	0.48734D-07	0.30553D-08
120.	0.39732D-06	0.10063D-06	0.30623D-08
130.	0.39619D-06	0.16424D-06	0.30698D-08
135.	0.39568D-06	0.19809D-06	0.30735D-08
150.	0.39441D-06	0.29563D-06	0.30836D-08
165.	0.39362D-06	0.36714D-06	0.30907D-08
180.	0.39334D-06	0.39334D-06	0.30932D-08

ALPHA = 0.60

THETA	SS	PP	SP
0.	0.46901D-05	0.46901D-05	0.34772D-07
5.	0.46893D-05	0.46531D-05	0.34769D-07
10.	0.46870D-05	0.45434D-05	0.34760D-07
20.	0.46778D-05	0.41229D-05	0.34725D-07
30.	0.46628D-05	0.34845D-05	0.34675D-07
40.	0.46424D-05	0.27113D-05	0.34618D-07
45.	0.46303D-05	0.23045D-05	0.34592D-07
50.	0.46172D-05	0.19010D-05	0.34568D-07
60.	0.45881D-05	0.11524D-05	0.34535D-07
70.	0.45559D-05	0.55246D-06	0.34531D-07
80.	0.45215D-05	0.16683D-06	0.34565D-07
90.	0.44861D-05	0.33955D-07	0.34640D-07
100.	0.44507D-05	0.16257D-06	0.34757D-07
110.	0.44163D-05	0.53233D-06	0.34910D-07
120.	0.43841D-05	0.10967D-05	0.35089D-07
130.	0.43549D-05	0.17879D-05	0.35280D-07
135.	0.43418D-05	0.21558D-05	0.35375D-07
150.	0.43094D-05	0.32167D-05	0.35634D-07
165.	0.42890D-05	0.39961D-05	0.35815D-07
180.	0.42821D-05	0.42821D-05	0.35880D-07

ALPHA = 0.80

THETA	SS	PP	SP
0.	0.26575D-04	0.26575D-04	0.19562D-06
5.	0.26567D-04	0.26358D-04	0.19559D-06
10.	0.26544D-04	0.25716D-04	0.19549D-06
20.	0.26452D-04	0.23263D-04	0.19515D-06
30.	0.26302D-04	0.19563D-04	0.19465D-06
40.	0.26098D-04	0.15123D-04	0.19408D-06
45.	0.25978D-04	0.12806D-04	0.19381D-06
50.	0.25847D-04	0.10523D-04	0.19358D-06
60.	0.25556D-04	0.63291D-05	0.19325D-06
70.	0.25234D-04	0.30129D-05	0.19321D-06
80.	0.24891D-04	0.90800D-06	0.19355D-06
90.	0.24537D-04	0.18745D-06	0.19430D-06
100.	0.24183D-04	0.86546D-06	0.19547D-06
110.	0.23840D-04	0.28118D-05	0.19700D-06
120.	0.23518D-04	0.57724D-05	0.19878D-06
130.	0.23227D-04	0.93934D-05	0.20069D-06
135.	0.23096D-04	0.11321D-04	0.20164D-06
150.	0.22772D-04	0.16888D-04	0.20423D-06
165.	0.22569D-04	0.20991D-04	0.20604D-06
180.	0.22499D-04	0.22499D-04	0.20668D-06

ALPHA = 1.00

THETA	SS	PP	SP
0.	0.10247D-03	0.10247D-03	0.74742D-06
5.	0.10242D-03	0.10160D-03	0.74724D-06
10.	0.10228D-03	0.99022D-04	0.74669D-06
20.	0.10173D-03	0.89221D-04	0.74464D-06
30.	0.10084D-03	0.74550D-04	0.74164D-06
40.	0.99625D-04	0.57143D-04	0.73827D-06
45.	0.98909D-04	0.48156D-04	0.73667D-06
50.	0.98128D-04	0.39369D-04	0.73525D-06
60.	0.96393D-04	0.23428D-04	0.73330D-06
70.	0.94475D-04	0.11046D-04	0.73308D-06
80.	0.92430D-04	0.33197D-05	0.73509D-06
90.	0.90320D-04	0.69877D-06	0.73959D-06
100.	0.88211D-04	0.30661D-05	0.74654D-06
110.	0.86166D-04	0.98475D-05	0.75564D-06
120.	0.84247D-04	0.20110D-04	0.76628D-06
130.	0.82513D-04	0.32634D-04	0.77765D-06
135.	0.81732D-04	0.39302D-04	0.78332D-06
150.	0.79802D-04	0.58609D-04	0.79876D-06
165.	0.78588D-04	0.72901D-04	0.80953D-06
180.	0.78174D-04	0.78174D-04	0.81339D-06

ALPHA = 0.10

THETA	SS	PP	SP
0.	0.68254D-10	0.68254D-10	0.26034D-14
5.	0.68253D-10	0.67734D-10	0.26034D-14
10.	0.68252D-10	0.66192D-10	0.26034D-14
20.	0.68245D-10	0.60258D-10	0.26035D-14
30.	0.68235D-10	0.51169D-10	0.26037D-14
40.	0.68222D-10	0.40025D-10	0.26040D-14
45.	0.68214D-10	0.34098D-10	0.26042D-14
50.	0.68205D-10	0.28172D-10	0.26044D-14
60.	0.68185D-10	0.17041D-10	0.26049D-14
70.	0.68164D-10	0.79721D-11	0.26055D-14
80.	0.68141D-10	0.20563D-11	0.26062D-14
90.	0.68117D-10	0.26059D-14	0.26070D-14
100.	0.68094D-10	0.20541D-11	0.26079D-14
110.	0.68071D-10	0.79596D-11	0.26088D-14
120.	0.68049D-10	0.17005D-10	0.26097D-14
130.	0.68030D-10	0.28058D-10	0.26106D-14
135.	0.68021D-10	0.34000D-10	0.26110D-14
150.	0.67999D-10	0.50591D-10	0.26120D-14
165.	0.67986D-10	0.63429D-10	0.26127D-14
180.	0.67981D-10	0.67981D-10	0.26129D-14

ALPHA = 0.20

THETA	SS	PP	SP
0.	0.43709D-08	0.43709D-08	0.16577D-12
5.	0.43708D-08	0.43375D-08	0.16578D-12
10.	0.43704D-08	0.42383D-08	0.16578D-12
20.	0.43688D-08	0.38567D-08	0.16582D-12
30.	0.43663D-08	0.32727D-08	0.16587D-12
40.	0.43628D-08	0.25577D-08	0.16594D-12
45.	0.43607D-08	0.21778D-08	0.16599D-12
50.	0.43585D-08	0.17984D-08	0.16604D-12
60.	0.43535D-08	0.10866D-08	0.16617D-12
70.	0.43480D-08	0.50777D-09	0.16633D-12
80.	0.43421D-08	0.13086D-09	0.16651D-12
90.	0.43360D-08	0.16643D-12	0.16671D-12
100.	0.43300D-08	0.13028D-09	0.16694D-12
110.	0.43241D-08	0.50458D-09	0.16717D-12
120.	0.43186D-08	0.10774D-08	0.16740D-12
130.	0.43136D-08	0.17793D-08	0.16762D-12
135.	0.43113D-08	0.21526D-08	0.16772D-12
150.	0.43058D-08	0.32271D-08	0.16799D-12
165.	0.43023D-08	0.40133D-08	0.16816D-12
180.	0.43011D-08	0.43011D-08	0.16823D-12

ALPHA = 0.40

THETA	SS	PP	SP
0.	0.28043D-06	0.28043D-06	0.10394D-10
5.	0.28040D-06	0.27825D-06	0.10395D-10
10.	0.28030D-06	0.27176D-06	0.10397D-10
20.	0.27989D-06	0.24687D-06	0.10405D-10
30.	0.27923D-06	0.20891D-06	0.10418D-10
40.	0.27834D-06	0.16268D-06	0.10438D-10
45.	0.27781D-06	0.13823D-06	0.10450D-10
50.	0.27724D-06	0.11390D-06	0.10464D-10
60.	0.27596D-06	0.68509D-07	0.10496D-10
70.	0.27455D-06	0.31872D-07	0.10536D-10
80.	0.27305D-06	0.81856D-08	0.10583D-10
90.	0.27149D-06	0.10562D-10	0.10635D-10
100.	0.26994D-06	0.80355D-08	0.10692D-10
110.	0.26844D-06	0.31055D-07	0.10751D-10
120.	0.26703D-06	0.66149D-07	0.10810D-10
130.	0.26575D-06	0.10903D-06	0.10867D-10
135.	0.26517D-06	0.13180D-06	0.10893D-10
150.	0.26375D-06	0.19723D-06	0.10961D-10
165.	0.26286D-06	0.24506D-06	0.11006D-10
180.	0.26256D-06	0.26256D-06	0.11022D-10

ALPHA = 0.60

THETA	SS	PP	SP
0.	0.32074D-05	0.32074D-05	0.11432D-09
5.	0.32065D-05	0.31816D-05	0.11433D-09
10.	0.32039D-05	0.31052D-05	0.11438D-09
20.	0.31936D-05	0.28127D-05	0.11458D-09
30.	0.31767D-05	0.23693D-05	0.11492D-09
40.	0.31538D-05	0.18338D-05	0.11542D-09
45.	0.31403D-05	0.15529D-05	0.11573D-09
50.	0.31256D-05	0.12748D-05	0.11609D-09
60.	0.30929D-05	0.76076D-06	0.11693D-09
70.	0.30567D-05	0.35116D-06	0.11795D-09
80.	0.30181D-05	0.89637D-07	0.11914D-09
90.	0.29784D-05	0.11860D-09	0.12048D-09
100.	0.29386D-05	0.85791D-07	0.12193D-09
110.	0.29000D-05	0.33024D-06	0.12345D-09
120.	0.28638D-05	0.70027D-06	0.12497D-09
130.	0.28311D-05	0.11499D-05	0.12642D-09
135.	0.28164D-05	0.13879D-05	0.12710D-09
150.	0.27800D-05	0.20699D-05	0.12885D-09
165.	0.27571D-05	0.25674D-05	0.12999D-09
180.	0.27493D-05	0.27493D-05	0.13039D-09

P = 2.00   M = 1.05

ALPHA = 0.80

THETA	SS	PP	SP
0.	0.18125D-04	0.18125D-04	0.61019D-09
5.	0.18116D-04	0.17973D-04	0.61035D-09
10.	0.18090D-04	0.17524D-04	0.61084D-09
20.	0.17987D-04	0.15809D-04	0.61284D-09
30.	0.17818D-04	0.13232D-04	0.61626D-09
40.	0.17589D-04	0.10153D-04	0.62123D-09
45.	0.17454D-04	0.85541D-05	0.62433D-09
50.	0.17307D-04	0.69846D-05	0.62787D-09
60.	0.16981D-04	0.41203D-05	0.63627D-09
70.	0.16619D-04	0.18797D-05	0.64646D-09
80.	0.16234D-04	0.47531D-06	0.65836D-09
90.	0.15837D-04	0.65298D-09	0.67174D-09
100.	0.15439D-04	0.43689D-06	0.68624D-09
110.	0.15054D-04	0.16707D-05	0.70139D-09
120.	0.14693D-04	0.35161D-05	0.71657D-09
130.	0.14366D-04	0.57369D-05	0.73110D-09
135.	0.14219D-04	0.69059D-05	0.73789D-09
150.	0.13855D-04	0.10241D-04	0.75534D-09
165.	0.13627D-04	0.12664D-04	0.76679D-09
180.	0.13549D-04	0.13549D-04	0.77078D-09

ALPHA = 1.00

THETA	SS	PP	SP
0.	0.69646D-04	0.69646D-04	0.21701D-08
5.	0.69594D-04	0.69034D-04	0.21711D-08
10.	0.69439D-04	0.67221D-04	0.21740D-08
20.	0.68824D-04	0.60337D-04	0.21859D-08
30.	0.67819D-04	0.50077D-04	0.22063D-08
40.	0.66456D-04	0.37989D-04	0.22359D-08
45.	0.65652D-04	0.31793D-04	0.22544D-08
50.	0.64775D-04	0.25771D-04	0.22755D-08
60.	0.62828D-04	0.14961D-04	0.23256D-08
70.	0.60674D-04	0.67122D-05	0.23864D-08
80.	0.58378D-04	0.16742D-05	0.24573D-08
90.	0.56010D-04	0.24252D-08	0.25370D-08
100.	0.53641D-04	0.14452D-05	0.26235D-08
110.	0.51345D-04	0.54665D-05	0.27138D-08
120.	0.49191D-04	0.11360D-04	0.28043D-08
130.	0.47244D-04	0.18334D-04	0.28908D-08
135.	0.46367D-04	0.21970D-04	0.29313D-08
150.	0.44200D-04	0.32252D-04	0.30353D-08
165.	0.42837D-04	0.39670D-04	0.31036D-08
180.	0.42373D-04	0.42373D-04	0.31274D-08

ALPHA = 0.10

THETA	SS	PP	SP
0.	0.26792D-09	0.26792D-09	0.40711D-13
5.	0.26792D-09	0.26588D-09	0.40711D-13
10.	0.26791D-09	0.25983D-09	0.40711D-13
20.	0.26789D-09	0.23654D-09	0.40713D-13
30.	0.26785D-09	0.20087D-09	0.40716D-13
40.	0.26780D-09	0.15713D-09	0.40720D-13
45.	0.26777D-09	0.13387D-09	0.40723D-13
50.	0.26773D-09	0.11061D-09	0.40726D-13
60.	0.26765D-09	0.66919D-10	0.40733D-13
70.	0.26757D-09	0.31324D-10	0.40742D-13
80.	0.26748D-09	0.81033D-11	0.40752D-13
90.	0.26739D-09	0.40747D-13	0.40764D-13
100.	0.26729D-09	0.80910D-11	0.40777D-13
110.	0.26720D-09	0.31269D-10	0.40790D-13
120.	0.26712D-09	0.66770D-10	0.40804D-13
130.	0.26704D-09	0.11031D-09	0.40817D-13
135.	0.26701D-09	0.13347D-09	0.40823D-13
150.	0.26692D-09	0.20017D-09	0.40838D-13
165.	0.26687D-09	0.24898D-09	0.40849D-13
180.	0.26685D-09	0.26685D-09	0.40852D-13

ALPHA = 0.20

THETA	SS	PP	SP
0.	0.17168D-07	0.17168D-07	0.25964D-11
5.	0.17168D-07	0.17037D-07	0.25964D-11
10.	0.17166D-07	0.16647D-07	0.25965D-11
20.	0.17160D-07	0.15149D-07	0.25969D-11
30.	0.17150D-07	0.12856D-07	0.25977D-11
40.	0.17136D-07	0.10048D-07	0.25987D-11
45.	0.17128D-07	0.85560D-08	0.25994D-11
50.	0.17119D-07	0.70659D-08	0.26002D-11
60.	0.17100D-07	0.42704D-08	0.26020D-11
70.	0.17078D-07	0.19970D-08	0.26043D-11
80.	0.17055D-07	0.51635D-09	0.26070D-11
90.	0.17031D-07	0.26055D-11	0.26100D-11
100.	0.17007D-07	0.51320D-09	0.26133D-11
110.	0.16984D-07	0.19829D-08	0.26167D-11
120.	0.16963D-07	0.42323D-08	0.26201D-11
130.	0.16943D-07	0.69892D-08	0.26235D-11
135.	0.16934D-07	0.84554D-08	0.26250D-11
150.	0.16912D-07	0.12675D-07	0.26290D-11
165.	0.16899D-07	0.15764D-07	0.26316D-11
180.	0.16894D-07	0.16894D-07	0.26326D-11

ALPHA = 0.40

THETA	SS	PP	SP
0.	0.11042D-05	0.11042D-05	0.16383D-09
5.	0.11041D-05	0.10956D-05	0.16384D-09
10.	0.11037D-05	0.107C1D-05	0.16386D-09
20.	0.11021D-05	0.97214D-C6	0.16397D-09
30.	0.10995D-05	0.82280D-06	0.16416D-09
40.	0.10960D-05	0.64086D-06	0.16444D-09
45.	0.10939D-05	0.54464D-06	0.16461D-09
50.	0.10917D-05	0.44886D-06	0.16481D-09
60.	0.10866D-05	C.27013D-C6	0.16528D-09
70.	0.10811D-05	0.12582D-06	0.16586D-09
80.	0.10752D-C5	0.32467D-07	0.16655D-09
90.	0.10691D-05	0.16617D-09	0.16732D-09
100.	0.10630D-05	0.31661D-07	0.16815D-09
110.	0.10571D-05	0.12223D-06	0.16903D-09
120.	0.10515D-05	C.26038D-06	0.16992D-09
130.	0.10465D-05	0.42924D-06	0.17077D-09
135.	0.10443D-05	0.51850D-06	0.17116D-09
150.	0.10387D-05	0.77664D-06	0.17219D-09
165.	0.10352D-C5	0.96506D-06	0.17286D-09
180.	0.10340D-05	0.10340D-05	0.17309D-09

ALPHA = 0.60

THETA	SS	PP	SP
0.	0.12681D-04	0.12681D-04	0.18217D-08
5.	0.12677D-04	0.12579D-04	0.18219D-08
10.	0.12667D-04	0.12277D-04	0.18226D-08
20.	0.12626D-C4	0.11123D-04	0.18254D-08
30.	0.12560D-04	0.93728D-05	0.18302D-08
40.	0.12470D-04	0.72580D-05	0.18373D-08
45.	0.12417D-04	0.61480D-05	0.18418D-08
50.	0.12359D-04	0.50492D-05	0.18469D-08
60.	0.12231D-04	0.30167D-05	0.18590D-08
70.	0.12089D-04	0.13956D-C5	0.18739D-08
80.	0.11937D-04	0.35883D-06	0.18913D-08
90.	0.11781D-04	0.18817D-08	0.19111D-08
100.	0.11625D-04	0.33816D-06	0.19326D-08
110.	0.11473D-04	0.13034D-05	0.19551D-08
120.	0.11331D-04	0.27667D-C5	0.19778D-08
130.	0.11203D-04	0.45462D-05	0.19995D-08
135.	0.11145D-04	0.54883D-05	0.20097D-08
150.	0.11002D-04	0.81858D-05	0.20359D-08
165.	0.10912D-04	0.10161D-04	0.20532D-08
180.	0.10881D-04	0.10881D-C4	0.20592D-08

ALPHA = 0.80

THETA	SS	PP	SP
0.	0.72059D-04	0.72059D-04	0.98857D-08
5.	0.72024D-04	0.71458D-04	0.98880D-08
10.	0.71922D-04	0.69678D-04	0.98949D-08
20.	0.71517D-04	0.62886D-04	0.99230D-08
30.	0.70855D-04	0.52667D-04	0.99714D-08
40.	0.69956D-04	0.40452D-04	0.10042D-07
45.	0.69427D-04	0.34104D-04	0.10087D-07
50.	0.68849D-04	0.27869D-04	0.10138D-07
60.	0.67566D-04	0.16475D-04	0.10259D-07
70.	0.66146D-04	0.75452D-05	0.10408D-07
80.	0.64633D-04	0.19296D-05	0.10582D-07
90.	0.63073D-04	0.10486D-07	0.10779D-07
100.	0.61513D-04	0.17232D-05	0.10994D-07
110.	0.60000D-04	0.66247D-05	0.11219D-07
120.	0.58580D-04	0.13979D-04	0.11445D-07
130.	0.57297D-04	0.22844D-04	0.11663D-07
135.	0.56720D-04	0.27515D-04	0.11764D-07
150.	0.55292D-04	0.40850D-04	0.12026D-07
165.	0.54394D-04	0.50546D-04	0.12198D-07
180.	0.54088D-04	0.54088D-04	0.12258D-07

ALPHA = 1.00

THETA	SS	PP	SP
0.	0.27886D-03	0.27886D-03	0.35997D-07
5.	0.27865D-03	0.27642D-03	0.36011D-07
10.	0.27804D-03	0.26921D-03	0.36052D-07
20.	0.27563D-03	0.24181D-03	0.36219D-07
30.	0.27168D-03	0.20093D-03	0.36508D-07
40.	0.26633D-03	0.15270D-03	0.36930D-07
45.	0.26317D-03	0.12794D-03	0.37195D-07
50.	0.25973D-03	0.10385D-03	0.37498D-07
60.	0.25208D-03	0.60522D-04	0.38222D-07
70.	0.24362D-03	0.27330D-04	0.39107D-07
80.	0.23460D-03	0.69369D-05	0.40146D-07
90.	0.22530D-03	0.39574D-07	0.41321D-07
100.	0.21600D-03	0.57063D-05	0.42601D-07
110.	0.20698D-03	0.21844D-04	0.43944D-07
120.	0.19852D-03	0.45642D-04	0.45293D-07
130.	0.19088D-03	0.73906D-04	0.46588D-07
135.	0.18743D-03	0.88668D-04	0.47194D-07
150.	0.17892D-03	0.13050D-03	0.48754D-07
165.	0.17357D-03	0.16072D-03	0.49780D-07
180.	0.17174D-03	0.17174D-03	0.50138D-07

P = 2.00

M = 1.20

ALPHA = 0.10

THETA	SS	PP	SP
0.	0.10282D-08	0.10282D-08	0.61578D-12
5.	0.10281D-08	0.102C3D-08	0.61578D-12
10.	0.10281D-08	0.99713D-09	0.61578D-12
20.	0.10280D-08	0.90780D-09	0.61580D-12
30.	0.10279D-08	0.77097D-09	0.61584D-12
40.	0.10277D-08	0.60321D-C9	0.61589D-12
45.	0.10276D-08	0.51397D-09	0.61593D-12
50.	0.10274D-08	0.42476D-09	0.61596D-12
60.	0.10271D-08	0.25718D-09	0.61606D-12
70.	0.10268D-08	0.12063D-09	0.61617D-12
80.	0.10264D-08	0.31555D-10	0.61631D-12
90.	0.10261D-08	0.61621D-12	0.61647D-12
100.	0.10257D-08	0.31483D-10	0.61665D-12
110.	0.10254D-C8	0.12038D-09	0.61683D-12
120.	0.10251D-C8	0.25655D-C9	0.61702D-12
130.	0.10248D-08	0.42355D-09	0.61720D-12
135.	0.10246D-08	0.51241D-09	0.61728D-12
150.	0.10243D-08	0.76822D-09	0.61750D-12
165.	0.10241D-08	0.95548D-C9	0.61764D-12
180.	0.10240D-08	0.10240D-08	0.61769D-12

ALPHA = 0.2C

THETA	SS	PP	SP
0.	0.65964D-07	0.65964D-07	0.39388D-10
5.	0.65962D-07	0.65461D-07	C.39388D-10
10.	0.65956D-07	0.63965D-07	0.39389D-10
20.	0.65933D-07	0.58211D-07	0.39394D-10
30.	0.65894D-07	0.494C7D-07	0.39404D-10
40.	0.65841D-07	0.38625D-C7	0.39417D-10
45.	0.65810D-07	0.32896D-07	0.39426D-10
50.	0.65776D-07	0.27174D-07	0.39436D-10
60.	0.65700D-07	0.16438D-C7	0.39460D-10
70.	0.65616D-07	0.77048D-C8	0.39489D-10
80.	0.65527D-07	0.20158D-C8	0.39525D-10
90.	0.65436D-07	0.39498D-10	0.39565D-10
100.	0.65344D-C7	0.19973D-C8	0.39610D-10
110.	0.65255D-07	0.76593D-C8	0.39657D-10
120.	0.65171D-C7	0.16277D-07	0.39705D-10
130.	0.65C96D-07	0.26864D-07	0.39751D-10
135.	0.65062D-07	0.32495D-07	0.39773D-10
150.	0.64978D-07	0.48703D-07	0.39829D-10
165.	0.64925D-07	0.60565D-07	C.39866D-10
180.	0.64907D-07	0.649C7D-07	0.39879D-10

ALPHA = 0.40

THETA	SS	PP	SP
0.	0.42633D-05	0.42633D-05	0.25151D-08
5.	0.42628D-05	0.42302D-05	0.25152D-08
10.	0.42613D-05	0.41319D-05	0.25156D-08
20.	0.42552D-05	0.37543D-05	0.25169D-08
30.	0.42452D-05	0.31786D-05	0.25192D-08
40.	0.42316D-05	0.24770D-05	0.25227D-08
45.	0.42237D-05	0.21059D-05	0.25249D-08
50.	0.42150D-05	0.17363D-05	0.25274D-08
60.	0.41956D-05	0.10465D-05	0.25336D-08
70.	0.41742D-05	0.48908D-06	0.25412D-08
80.	0.41514D-05	0.12805D-06	0.25503D-08
90.	0.41279D-05	0.25434D-08	0.25607D-08
100.	0.41044D-05	0.12332D-06	0.25721D-08
110.	0.40816D-05	0.47231D-06	0.25842D-08
120.	0.40602D-05	0.10052D-05	0.25964D-08
130.	0.40409D-05	0.16570D-05	0.26082D-08
135.	0.40322D-05	0.20032D-05	0.26138D-08
150.	0.40107D-05	0.29985D-05	0.26281D-08
165.	0.39972D-05	0.37263D-05	0.26375D-08
180.	0.39925D-05	0.39925D-05	0.26408D-08

ALPHA = 0.60

THETA	SS	PP	SP
0.	0.49352D-04	0.49352D-04	0.28541D-07
5.	0.49338D-04	0.48958D-04	0.28544D-07
10.	0.49299D-04	0.47789D-04	0.28552D-07
20.	0.49142D-04	0.43311D-04	0.28587D-07
30.	0.48887D-04	0.36521D-04	0.28646D-07
40.	0.48540D-04	0.28310D-04	0.28735D-07
45.	0.48335D-04	0.23997D-04	0.28791D-07
50.	0.48112D-04	0.19725D-04	0.28856D-07
60.	0.47617D-04	0.11815D-04	0.29014D-07
70.	0.47069D-04	0.54944D-05	0.29209D-07
80.	0.46484D-04	0.14403D-05	0.29442D-07
90.	0.45882D-04	0.29265D-07	0.29708D-07
100.	0.45279D-04	0.13192D-05	0.30002D-07
110.	0.44695D-04	0.50646D-05	0.30311D-07
120.	0.44147D-04	0.10758D-04	0.30625D-07
130.	0.43651D-04	0.17691D-04	0.30927D-07
135.	0.43428D-04	0.21365D-04	0.31069D-07
150.	0.42877D-04	0.31904D-04	0.31436D-07
165.	0.42530D-04	0.39598D-04	0.31678D-07
180.	0.42412D-04	0.42412D-04	0.31762D-07

ALPHA = 0.80

THETA	SS	PP	SP
0.	0.28350D-03	0.28350D-03	0.15952D-06
5.	0.28337D-03	0.28116D-03	0.15954D-06
10.	0.28298D-03	0.27420D-03	0.15963D-06
20.	0.28141D-03	0.24766D-03	0.15997D-06
30.	0.27986D-03	0.20767D-03	0.16056D-06
40.	0.27539D-03	0.15981D-03	0.16145D-06
45.	0.27335D-03	0.13490D-03	0.16201D-06
50.	0.27112D-03	0.11041D-03	0.16266D-06
60.	0.26617D-03	0.65553D-04	0.16424D-06
70.	0.26070D-03	0.30269D-04	0.16619D-06
80.	0.25486D-03	0.79955D-05	0.16852D-06
90.	0.24884D-03	0.16675D-06	0.17118D-06
100.	0.24282D-03	0.67389D-05	0.17410D-06
110.	0.23699D-03	0.25976D-04	0.17720D-06
120.	0.23151D-03	0.55001D-04	0.18033D-06
130.	0.22656D-03	0.90097D-04	0.18335D-06
135.	0.22433D-03	0.10862D-03	0.18477D-06
150.	0.21883D-03	0.16156D-03	0.18843D-06
165.	0.21536D-03	0.20010D-03	0.19085D-06
180.	0.21418D-03	0.21418D-03	0.19169D-06

ALPHA = 1.00

THETA	SS	PP	SP
0.	0.11119D-02	0.11119D-02	0.60435D-06
5.	0.11112D-02	0.11023D-02	0.60452D-06
10.	0.11088D-02	0.10739D-02	0.60501D-06
20.	0.10995D-02	0.96583D-03	0.60705D-06
30.	0.10843D-02	0.80434D-03	0.61060D-06
40.	0.10636D-02	0.61330D-03	0.61588D-06
45.	0.10514D-02	0.51499D-03	0.61924D-06
50.	0.10381D-02	0.41911D-03	0.62312D-06
60.	0.10086D-02	0.24600D-03	0.63250D-06
70.	0.97601D-03	0.11251D-03	0.64414D-06
80.	0.94123D-03	0.29622D-04	0.65799D-06
90.	0.90535D-03	0.64745D-06	0.67385D-06
100.	0.86948D-03	0.22406D-04	0.69129D-06
110.	0.83469D-03	0.86924D-04	0.70973D-06
120.	0.80206D-03	0.18311D-03	0.72839D-06
130.	0.77256D-03	0.29806D-03	0.74639D-06
135.	0.75927D-03	0.35830D-03	0.75485D-06
150.	0.72644D-03	0.52948D-03	0.77669D-06
165.	0.70580D-03	0.65350D-03	0.79110D-06
180.	0.69876D-03	0.69876D-03	0.79613D-06

ALPHA = 0.10

THETA	SS	PP	SP
0.	0.22105D-08	0.221C5D-08	0.29127D-11
5.	0.22105D-08	0.21937D-08	0.29127D-11
10.	0.22104D-08	0.21438D-C8	0.29127D-11
20.	0.22102D-08	0.19519D-C8	0.29128D-11
30.	0.22099D-08	0.16580D-C8	0.29129D-11
40.	0.22094D-08	0.12976D-08	0.29131D-11
45.	0.22092D-08	0.11C59D-C8	0.29133D-11
50.	0.22089D-08	0.91421D-09	0.29134D-11
60.	0.22082D-08	0.55416D-09	0.29138D-11
70.	0.22075D-08	0.26081D-09	0.29143D-11
80.	0.22068D-08	0.69409D-10	0.29149D-11
90.	0.22060D-08	0.29143D-11	0.29156D-11
100.	0.22052D-08	0.69201D-10	0.29163D-11
110.	0.22044D-08	0.26016D-C9	0.29171D-11
120.	0.22037D-08	0.55268D-09	0.29179D-11
130.	0.22031D-08	0.91146D-09	0.29187D-11
135.	0.22028D-08	C.11023D-08	0.29191D-11
150.	0.22021D-08	0.16519D-C8	0.29200D-11
165.	0.22016D-08	0.20542D-C8	0.29207D-11
180.	0.22015D-08	0.22015D-C8	0.29209D-11

ALPHA = 0.20

THETA	SS	PP	SP
0.	0.14199D-06	0.14199D-06	0.18683D-09
5.	0.14199D-06	0.14091D-06	0.18683D-09
10.	0.14197D-06	0.13769D-06	0.18683D-09
20.	0.14192D-06	0.12532D-06	0.18685D-09
30.	0.14184D-06	0.10639D-06	0.18689D-09
40.	0.14172D-06	0.83197D-07	0.18694D-09
45.	0.14166D-06	0.70877D-07	0.18697D-09
50.	0.14158D-06	0.58569D-07	0.18701D-09
60.	0.14142D-06	0.35475D-07	0.18711D-09
70.	0.14124D-06	0.16687D-07	0.18723D-09
80.	0.14104D-06	0.44449D-C8	0.18738D-09
90.	0.14084D-06	0.18724D-09	0.18756D-09
100.	0.14064D-06	0.43916D-08	0.18775D-09
110.	0.14045D-06	0.16522D-07	0.18795D-09
120.	0.14027D-06	0.35096D-07	0.18816D-09
130.	0.14011D-06	0.57867D-07	0.18836D-09
135.	0.14003D-06	0.69978D-07	0.18846D-09
150.	0.13985D-06	0.10484D-06	0.18870D-09
165.	0.13973D-06	0.13036D-06	0.18887D-09
180.	0.13970D-06	0.13970D-06	0.18892D-09

ALPHA = 0.40

THETA	SS	PP	SP
0.	0.92211D-05	0.92211D-05	0.12063D-07
5.	0.92200D-05	0.91496D-05	0.12063D-07
10.	0.92167D-05	0.89374D-05	0.12064D-07
20.	0.92034D-05	0.81224D-05	0.12069D-07
30.	0.91818D-05	0.68793D-05	0.12078D-07
40.	0.91524D-05	0.53639D-05	0.12092D-07
45.	0.91350D-05	0.45622D-05	0.12101D-07
50.	0.91161D-05	0.37637D-05	0.12111D-07
60.	0.90741D-05	0.22725D-05	0.12136D-07
70.	0.90277D-05	0.10669D-05	0.12167D-07
80.	0.89782D-05	0.28517D-06	0.12205D-07
90.	0.89271D-05	0.12168D-07	0.12249D-07
100.	0.88761D-05	0.27154D-06	0.12299D-07
110.	0.88266D-05	0.10245D-05	0.12351D-07
120.	0.87801D-05	0.21755D-05	0.12404D-07
130.	0.87381D-05	0.35839D-05	0.12456D-07
135.	0.87192D-05	0.43321D-05	0.12480D-07
150.	0.86725D-05	0.64838D-05	0.12543D-07
165.	0.86431D-05	0.80573D-05	0.12585D-07
180.	0.86331D-05	0.86331D-05	0.12600D-07

ALPHA = 0.60

THETA	SS	PP	SP
0.	0.10757D-03	0.10757D-03	0.13941D-06
5.	0.10754D-03	0.10672D-03	0.13942D-06
10.	0.10746D-03	0.10418D-03	0.13946D-06
20.	0.10712D-03	0.94454D-04	0.13958D-06
30.	0.10656D-03	0.79698D-04	0.13981D-06
40.	0.10581D-03	0.61845D-04	0.14016D-06
45.	0.10536D-03	0.52460D-04	0.14038D-06
50.	0.10488D-03	0.43161D-04	0.14064D-06
60.	0.10380D-03	0.25926D-04	0.14128D-06
70.	0.10261D-03	0.12133D-04	0.14209D-06
80.	0.10135D-03	0.32615D-05	0.14307D-06
90.	0.10004D-03	0.14210D-06	0.14420D-06
100.	0.98728D-04	0.29121D-05	0.14545D-06
110.	0.97460D-04	0.11045D-04	0.14679D-06
120.	0.96269D-04	0.23440D-04	0.14816D-06
130.	0.95193D-04	0.38553D-04	0.14948D-06
135.	0.94709D-04	0.46565D-04	0.15011D-06
150.	0.93511D-04	0.69562D-04	0.15172D-06
165.	0.92758D-04	0.86358D-04	0.15280D-06
180.	0.92502D-04	0.92502D-04	0.15317D-06

ALPHA = 0.80

THETA	SS	PP	SP
0.	0.62437D-03	0.62437D-03	0.79914D-06
5.	0.62408D-03	0.61923D-03	0.79924D-06
10.	0.62322D-03	0.60402D-03	0.79955D-06
20.	0.61983D-03	0.54592D-03	0.80083D-06
30.	0.61428D-03	0.45833D-03	0.80311D-06
40.	0.60676D-03	0.35335D-03	0.80656D-06
45.	0.60232D-03	0.29865D-03	0.80880D-06
50.	0.59748D-03	0.24479D-03	0.81140D-06
60.	0.58673D-03	0.14599D-03	0.81779D-06
70.	0.57484D-03	0.68014D-04	0.82586D-06
80.	0.56217D-03	0.18429D-04	0.83561D-06
90.	0.54910D-03	0.82598D-06	0.84691D-06
100.	0.53603D-03	0.14940D-04	0.85947D-06
110.	0.52336D-03	0.57148D-04	0.87286D-06
120.	0.51147D-03	0.12116D-03	0.88649D-06
130.	0.50072D-03	0.19876D-03	0.89972D-06
135.	0.49588D-03	0.23975D-03	0.90595D-06
150.	0.48392D-03	0.35709D-03	0.92210D-06
165.	0.47640D-03	0.44258D-03	0.93280D-06
180.	0.47384D-03	0.47384D-03	0.93654D-06

ALPHA = 1.00

THETA	SS	PP	SP
0.	0.24797D-02	0.24797D-02	0.31261D-05
5.	0.24780D-02	0.24585D-02	0.31267D-05
10.	0.24728D-02	0.23958D-02	0.31285D-05
20.	0.24526D-02	0.21572D-02	0.31362D-05
30.	0.24196D-02	0.18001D-02	0.31497D-05
40.	0.23747D-02	0.13767D-02	0.31703D-05
45.	0.23483D-02	0.11583D-02	0.31836D-05
50.	0.23194D-02	0.94497D-03	0.31991D-05
60.	0.22554D-02	0.55847D-03	0.32372D-05
70.	0.21845D-02	0.25868D-03	0.32853D-05
80.	0.21089D-02	0.70811D-04	0.33435D-05
90.	0.20310D-02	0.32861D-05	0.34108D-05
100.	0.19531D-02	0.50013D-04	0.34857D-05
110.	0.18776D-02	0.19391D-03	0.35654D-05
120.	0.18067D-02	0.41046D-03	0.36467D-05
130.	0.17427D-02	0.67061D-03	0.37255D-05
135.	0.17138D-02	0.80730D-03	0.37627D-05
150.	0.16425D-02	0.11966D-02	0.38590D-05
165.	0.15977D-02	0.14792D-02	0.39227D-05
180.	0.15824D-02	0.15824D-02	0.39450D-05

ALPHA = 0.10

THETA	SS	PP	SP
0.	0.37438D-08	0.37438D-08	0.85201D-11
5.	0.37437D-08	0.37154D-08	0.85201D-11
10.	0.37436D-08	0.36310D-08	0.85201D-11
20.	0.37433D-08	0.33063D-08	0.85203D-11
30.	0.37427D-08	0.28090D-08	0.85206D-11
40.	0.37420D-08	0.21992D-08	0.85211D-11
45.	0.37415D-08	0.18748D-08	0.85214D-11
50.	0.37410D-08	0.15506D-08	0.85218D-11
60.	0.37399D-08	0.94135D-09	0.85228D-11
70.	0.37387D-08	0.44496D-09	0.85240D-11
80.	0.37374D-08	0.12108D-09	0.85255D-11
90.	0.37361D-08	0.85236D-11	0.85273D-11
100.	0.37347D-08	0.12064D-09	0.85293D-11
110.	0.37334D-08	0.44370D-09	0.85314D-11
120.	0.37322D-08	0.93862D-09	0.85336D-11
130.	0.37311D-08	0.15457D-08	0.85358D-11
135.	0.37306D-08	0.18686D-08	0.85368D-11
150.	0.37294D-08	0.27985D-08	0.85395D-11
165.	0.37286D-08	0.34792D-08	0.85412D-11
180.	0.37284D-08	0.37284D-08	0.85418D-11

ALPHA = 0.20

THETA	SS	PP	SP
0.	0.24077D-06	0.24077D-06	0.54792D-09
5.	0.24077D-06	0.23894D-06	0.54793D-09
10.	0.24074D-06	0.23349D-06	0.54794D-09
20.	0.24065D-06	0.21254D-06	0.54798D-09
30.	0.24051D-06	0.18047D-06	0.54806D-09
40.	0.24031D-06	0.14119D-06	0.54819D-09
45.	0.24020D-06	0.12032D-06	0.54827D-09
50.	0.24007D-06	0.99475D-07	0.54837D-09
60.	0.23979D-06	0.60352D-07	0.54862D-09
70.	0.23948D-06	0.28521D-07	0.54893D-09
80.	0.23914D-06	0.77726D-08	0.54932D-09
90.	0.23880D-06	0.54884D-09	0.54978D-09
100.	0.23846D-06	0.76595D-08	0.55029D-09
110.	0.23813D-06	0.28197D-07	0.55084D-09
120.	0.23781D-06	0.59653D-07	0.55140D-09
130.	0.23753D-06	0.98220D-07	0.55195D-09
135.	0.23741D-06	0.11874D-06	0.55221D-09
150.	0.23709D-06	0.17779D-06	0.55289D-09
165.	0.23690D-06	0.22101D-06	0.55334D-09
180.	0.23683D-06	0.23683D-06	0.55350D-09

P = 2.00   M = 1.40

ALPHA = 0.40

THETA	SS	PP	SP
0.	0.15710D-04	0.15710D-04	0.35743D-07
5.	0.15708D-04	0.15588D-04	0.35744D-07
10.	0.15702D-04	0.15227D-04	0.35746D-07
20.	0.15679D-04	0.13842D-04	0.35758D-07
30.	0.15642D-04	0.11728D-04	0.35779D-07
40.	0.15592D-04	0.91505D-05	0.35811D-07
45.	0.15562D-04	0.77865D-05	0.35832D-07
50.	0.15529D-04	0.64279D-05	0.35857D-07
60.	0.15457D-04	0.38897D-05	0.35920D-07
70.	0.15377D-04	0.18364D-05	0.36001D-07
80.	0.15292D-04	0.50349D-06	0.36101D-07
90.	0.15205D-04	0.35978D-07	0.36217D-07
100.	0.15117D-04	0.47454D-06	0.36348D-07
110.	0.15032D-04	0.17536D-05	0.36489D-07
120.	0.14952D-04	0.37108D-05	0.36634D-07
130.	0.14880D-04	0.61066D-05	0.36775D-07
135.	0.14848D-04	0.73797D-05	0.36841D-07
150.	0.14767D-04	0.11041D-04	0.37014D-07
165.	0.14717D-04	0.13720D-04	0.37129D-07
180.	0.14700D-04	0.14700D-04	0.37170D-07

ALPHA = 0.60

THETA	SS	PP	SP
0.	0.18464D-03	0.18464D-03	0.41996D-06
5.	0.18459D-03	0.18318D-03	0.41998D-06
10.	0.18445D-03	0.17884D-03	0.42005D-06
20.	0.18386D-03	0.16221D-03	0.42035D-06
30.	0.18291D-03	0.13696D-03	0.42088D-06
40.	0.18162D-03	0.10640D-03	0.42171D-06
45.	0.18085D-03	0.90321D-04	0.42226D-06
50.	0.18002D-03	0.74384D-04	0.42290D-06
60.	0.17817D-03	0.44822D-04	0.42451D-06
70.	0.17613D-03	0.21129D-04	0.42659D-06
80.	0.17395D-03	0.58500D-05	0.42913D-06
90.	0.17170D-03	0.42600D-06	0.43212D-06
100.	0.16945D-03	0.51078D-05	0.43548D-06
110.	0.16727D-03	0.19005D-04	0.43909D-06
120.	0.16523D-03	0.40236D-04	0.44280D-06
130.	0.16338D-03	0.66150D-04	0.44641D-06
135.	0.16255D-03	0.79896D-04	0.44811D-06
150.	0.16049D-03	0.11937D-03	0.45255D-06
165.	0.15920D-03	0.14821D-03	0.45550D-06
180.	0.15876D-03	0.15876D-03	0.45653D-06

P = 2.00   M = 1.40

ALPHA = 0.80

THETA	SS	PP	SP
0.	0.10823D-02	0.10823D-02	0.24605D-05
5.	0.10818D-02	0.10734D-02	0.24608D-05
10.	0.10803D-02	0.10472D-02	0.24615D-05
20.	0.10745D-02	0.94713D-03	0.24644D-05
30.	0.10650D-02	0.79610D-03	0.24697D-05
40.	0.10520D-02	0.61485D-03	0.24780D-05
45.	0.10444D-02	0.52029D-03	0.24834D-05
50.	0.10361D-02	0.42711D-03	0.24899D-05
60.	0.10176D-02	0.25590D-03	0.25060D-05
70.	0.99722D-03	0.12037D-03	0.25267D-05
80.	0.97545D-03	0.33772D-04	0.25521D-05
90.	0.95300D-03	0.25208D-05	0.25820D-05
100.	0.93055D-03	0.26360D-04	0.26156D-05
110.	0.90879D-03	0.99161D-04	0.26516D-05
120.	0.88836D-03	0.21008D-03	0.26886D-05
130.	0.86990D-03	0.34487D-03	0.27247D-05
135.	0.86159D-03	0.41616D-03	0.27417D-05
150.	0.84104D-03	0.62037D-03	0.27861D-05
165.	0.82813D-03	0.76928D-03	0.28155D-05
180.	0.82372D-03	0.82372D-03	0.28258D-05

ALPHA = 1.00

THETA	SS	PP	SP
0.	0.43485D-02	0.43485D-02	0.98811D-05
5.	0.43455D-02	0.43117D-02	0.98825D-05
10.	0.43368D-02	0.42028D-02	0.98866D-05
20.	0.43020D-02	0.37883D-02	0.99041D-05
30.	0.42452D-02	0.31671D-02	0.99358D-05
40.	0.41682D-02	0.24290D-02	0.99852D-05
45.	0.41228D-02	0.20476D-02	0.10018D-04
50.	0.40732D-02	0.16743D-02	0.10056D-04
60.	0.39632D-02	0.99606D-03	0.10152D-04
70.	0.38415D-02	0.46731D-03	0.10275D-04
80.	0.37117D-02	0.13326D-03	0.10427D-04
90.	0.35779D-02	0.10241D-04	0.10605D-04
100.	0.34441D-02	0.89078D-04	0.10805D-04
110.	0.33144D-02	0.34088D-03	0.11020D-04
120.	0.31926D-02	0.72300D-03	0.11241D-04
130.	0.30826D-02	0.11841D-02	0.11456D-04
135.	0.30330D-02	0.14269D-02	0.11557D-04
150.	0.29106D-02	0.21197D-02	0.11821D-04
165.	0.28336D-02	0.26233D-02	0.11997D-04
180.	0.28073D-02	0.28073D-02	0.12058D-04

ALPHA = 0.02

THETA	SS	PP	SP
0.	0.11159D-11	0.11159D-11	0.70163D-16
5.	0.11159D-11	0.11075D-11	0.70127D-16
10.	0.11159D-11	0.10824D-11	0.70020D-16
20.	0.11160D-11	0.98574D-12	0.69595D-16
30.	0.11162D-11	0.83765D-12	0.68901D-16
40.	0.11163D-11	0.65587D-12	0.67959D-16
45.	0.11164D-11	0.55909D-12	0.67404D-16
50.	0.11166D-11	0.46226D-12	0.66798D-16
60.	0.11168D-11	0.28013D-12	0.65452D-16
70.	0.11171D-11	0.13143D-12	0.63963D-16
80.	0.11174D-11	0.34141D-13	0.62376D-16
90.	0.11177D-11	0.60743D-16	0.60739D-16
100.	0.11180D-11	0.33390D-13	0.59102D-16
110.	0.11183D-11	0.13020D-12	0.57514D-16
120.	0.11186D-11	0.27886D-12	0.56024D-16
130.	0.11189D-11	0.46145D-12	0.54677D-16
135.	0.11190D-11	0.55874D-12	0.54070D-16
150.	0.11193D-11	0.83899D-12	0.52571D-16
165.	0.11194D-11	0.10443D-11	0.51629D-16
180.	0.11195D-11	0.11195D-11	0.51307D-16

ALPHA = 0.04

THETA	SS	PP	SP
0.	0.70982D-10	0.70982D-10	0.62978D-14
5.	0.70984D-10	0.70449D-10	0.62886D-14
10.	0.70989D-10	0.68867D-10	0.62611D-14
20.	0.71010D-10	0.62771D-10	0.61523D-14
30.	0.71044D-10	0.53416D-10	0.59747D-14
40.	0.71090D-10	0.41911D-10	0.57335D-14
45.	0.71117D-10	0.35775D-10	0.55914D-14
50.	0.71146D-10	0.29626D-10	0.54362D-14
60.	0.71212D-10	0.18031D-10	0.50918D-14
70.	0.71284D-10	0.85219D-11	0.47106D-14
80.	0.71362D-10	0.22550D-11	0.43044D-14
90.	0.71442D-10	0.38863D-14	0.38853D-14
100.	0.71521D-10	0.20628D-11	0.34661D-14
110.	0.71599D-10	0.82055D-11	0.30597D-14
120.	0.71671D-10	0.17707D-10	0.26782D-14
130.	0.71737D-10	0.29429D-10	0.23334D-14
135.	0.71766D-10	0.35686D-10	0.21781D-14
150.	0.71839D-10	0.53760D-10	0.17943D-14
165.	0.71885D-10	0.67034D-10	0.15530D-14
180.	0.71901D-10	0.71901D-10	0.14707D-14

ALPHA = 0.06

THETA	SS	PP	SP
0.	0.80025D-09	0.80025D-09	0.10605D-12
5.	0.80029D-09	0.79433D-09	0.10581D-12
10.	0.80043D-09	0.77676D-09	0.10511D-12
20.	0.80096D-09	0.70900D-09	0.10232D-12
30.	0.80183D-09	0.60477D-09	0.97766D-13
40.	0.80300D-09	0.47618D-09	0.91586D-13
45.	0.80370D-09	0.40737D-09	0.87943D-13
50.	0.80445D-09	0.33825D-09	0.83967D-13
60.	0.80614D-09	0.20733D-09	0.75139D-13
70.	0.80800D-09	0.99164D-10	0.65371D-13
80.	0.80998D-09	0.27014D-10	0.54958D-13
90.	0.81202D-09	0.44245D-13	0.44218D-13
100.	0.81407D-09	0.22090D-10	0.33475D-13
110.	0.81605D-09	0.91055D-10	0.23058D-13
120.	0.81791D-09	0.19904D-09	0.13282D-13
130.	0.81959D-09	0.33320D-09	0.44455D-14
135.	0.82035D-09	0.40510D-09	0.46459D-15
150.	0.82222D-09	0.61358D-09	
165.	0.82339D-09	0.76732D-09	
180.	0.82379D-09	0.82379D-09	

ALPHA = 0.08

THETA	SS	PP	SP
0.	0.44312D-08	0.44312D-08	0.86574D-12
5.	0.44316D-08	0.43992D-08	0.86339D-12
10.	0.44330D-08	0.43040D-08	0.85636D-12
20.	0.44383D-08	0.39364D-08	0.82851D-12
30.	0.44469D-08	0.33691D-08	0.78303D-12
40.	0.44587D-08	0.26659D-08	0.72130D-12
45.	0.44656D-08	0.22878D-08	0.68490D-12
50.	0.44732D-08	0.19067D-08	0.64519D-12
60.	0.44900D-08	0.11803D-08	0.55701D-12
70.	0.45085D-08	0.57364D-09	0.45943D-12
80.	0.45283D-08	0.16223D-09	0.35543D-12
90.	0.45488D-08	0.24841D-12	0.24814D-12
100.	0.45692D-08	0.11304D-09	0.14084D-12
110.	0.45890D-08	0.49264D-09	0.36786D-13
120.	0.46076D-08	0.10974D-08	
130.	0.46243D-08	0.18563D-08	
135.	0.46319D-08	0.22651D-08	
150.	0.46506D-08	0.34571D-08	
165.	0.46623D-08	0.43409D-08	
180.	0.46664D-08	0.46664D-08	

ALPHA = 0.02

THETA	SS	PP	SP
0.	0.43900D-11	0.43900D-11	0.92013D-15
5.	0.43900D-11	0.43567D-11	0.92012D-15
10.	0.43900D-11	0.42577D-11	0.92009D-15
20.	0.43899D-11	0.38766D-11	0.91999D-15
30.	0.43898D-11	0.32928D-11	0.91982D-15
40.	0.43896D-11	0.25766D-11	0.91958D-15
45.	0.43895D-11	0.21955D-11	0.91944D-15
50.	0.43894D-11	0.18145D-11	0.91929D-15
60.	0.43892D-11	0.10983D-11	0.91894D-15
70.	0.43889D-11	0.51443D-12	0.91856D-15
80.	0.43887D-11	0.13333D-12	0.91815D-15
90.	0.43884D-11	0.91779D-15	0.91773D-15
100.	0.43881D-11	0.13313D-12	0.91730D-15
110.	0.43878D-11	0.51397D-12	0.91688D-15
120.	0.43876D-11	0.10975D-11	0.91648D-15
130.	0.43873D-11	0.18132D-11	0.91612D-15
135.	0.43872D-11	0.21940D-11	0.91595D-15
150.	0.43870D-11	0.32904D-11	0.91554D-15
165.	0.43868D-11	0.40930D-11	0.91529D-15
180.	0.43867D-11	0.43867D-11	0.91520D-15

ALPHA = 0.04

THETA	SS	PP	SP
0.	0.28096D-09	0.28096D-09	0.59336D-13
5.	0.28096D-09	0.27882D-09	0.59334D-13
10.	0.28095D-09	0.27249D-09	0.59327D-13
20.	0.28093D-09	0.24810D-09	0.59300D-13
30.	0.28090D-09	0.21074D-09	0.59256D-13
40.	0.28086D-09	0.16491D-09	0.59195D-13
45.	0.28084D-09	0.14053D-09	0.59160D-13
50.	0.28081D-09	0.11614D-09	0.59120D-13
60.	0.28075D-09	0.70307D-10	0.59033D-13
70.	0.28068D-09	0.32940D-10	0.58935D-13
80.	0.28061D-09	0.85456D-11	0.58830D-13
90.	0.28054D-09	0.58737D-13	0.58721D-13
100.	0.28047D-09	0.84941D-11	0.58611D-13
110.	0.28040D-09	0.32822D-10	0.58503D-13
120.	0.28033D-09	0.70097D-10	0.58401D-13
130.	0.28027D-09	0.11581D-09	0.58309D-13
135.	0.28024D-09	0.14013D-09	0.58267D-13
150.	0.28018D-09	0.21014D-09	0.58162D-13
165.	0.28013D-09	0.26137D-09	0.58096D-13
180.	0.28012D-09	0.28012D-09	0.58074D-13

ALPHA = 0.06

THETA	SS	PP	SP
0.	0.32002D-08	0.32002D-08	0.68439D-12
5.	0.32002D-08	0.31759D-08	0.68433D-12
10.	0.32001D-08	0.31038D-08	0.68415D-12
20.	0.31996D-08	0.28261D-08	0.68346D-12
30.	0.31988D-08	0.24006D-08	0.68232D-12
40.	0.31977D-08	0.18787D-08	0.68077D-12
45.	0.31971D-08	0.16009D-08	0.67985D-12
50.	0.31964D-08	0.13232D-08	0.67885D-12
60.	0.31949D-08	0.80115D-09	0.67660D-12
70.	0.31932D-08	0.37553D-09	0.67410D-12
80.	0.31914D-08	0.97575D-10	0.67141D-12
90.	0.31895D-08	0.66903D-12	0.66862D-12
100.	0.31876D-08	0.96257D-10	0.66579D-12
110.	0.31858D-08	0.37251D-09	0.66303D-12
120.	0.31841D-08	0.79578D-09	0.66042D-12
130.	0.31826D-08	0.13148D-08	0.65804D-12
135.	0.31819D-08	0.15908D-08	0.65697D-12
150.	0.31802D-08	0.23851D-08	0.65429D-12
165.	0.31791D-08	0.29662D-08	0.65260D-12
180.	0.31788D-08	0.31788D-08	0.65202D-12

ALPHA = 0.08

THETA	SS	PP	SP
0.	0.17981D-07	0.17981D-07	0.39123D-11
5.	0.17980D-07	0.17844D-07	0.39117D-11
10.	0.17979D-07	0.17439D-07	0.39099D-11
20.	0.17974D-07	0.15879D-07	0.39030D-11
30.	0.17966D-07	0.13489D-07	0.38916D-11
40.	0.17956D-07	0.10557D-07	0.38761D-11
45.	0.17949D-07	0.89970D-08	0.38670D-11
50.	0.17942D-07	0.74367D-08	0.38569D-11
60.	0.17927D-07	0.45039D-08	0.38345D-11
70.	0.17910D-07	0.21125D-08	0.38095D-11
80.	0.17892D-07	0.55010D-09	0.37827D-11
90.	0.17873D-07	0.37589D-11	0.37547D-11
100.	0.17855D-07	0.53693D-09	0.37265D-11
110.	0.17837D-07	0.20823D-08	0.36990D-11
120.	0.17820D-07	0.44503D-08	0.36729D-11
130.	0.17805D-07	0.73527D-08	0.36491D-11
135.	0.17798D-07	0.88959D-08	0.36384D-11
150.	0.17781D-07	0.13335D-07	0.36116D-11
165.	0.17770D-07	0.16579D-07	0.35947D-11
180.	0.17766D-07	0.17766D-07	0.35890D-11

ALPHA = 0.02

THETA	SS	PP	SP
0.	0.16862D-10	0.16862D-10	0.13005D-13
5.	0.16862D-10	0.16734D-10	0.13005D-13
10.	0.16862D-10	0.16354D-10	0.13005D-13
20.	0.16862D-10	0.14891D-10	0.13005D-13
30.	0.16861D-10	0.12650D-10	0.13004D-13
40.	0.16860D-10	0.99006D-11	0.13004D-13
45.	0.16860D-10	0.84377D-11	0.13003D-13
50.	0.16860D-10	0.69748D-11	0.13003D-13
60.	0.16859D-10	0.42255D-11	0.13002D-13
70.	0.16858D-10	0.19843D-11	0.13000D-13
80.	0.16856D-10	0.52130D-12	0.12999D-13
90.	0.16855D-10	0.12999D-13	0.12998D-13
100.	0.16854D-10	0.52052D-12	0.12996D-13
110.	0.16853D-10	0.19825D-11	0.12995D-13
120.	0.16852D-10	0.42223D-11	0.12993D-13
130.	0.16851D-10	0.69697D-11	0.12992D-13
135.	0.16851D-10	0.84315D-11	0.12991D-13
150.	0.16849D-10	0.12640D-10	0.12990D-13
165.	0.16849D-10	0.15721D-10	0.12989D-13
180.	0.16849D-10	0.16849D-10	0.12988D-13

ALPHA = 0.04

THETA	SS	PP	SP
0.	0.10796D-08	0.10796D-08	0.83405D-12
5.	0.10796D-08	0.10714D-08	0.83404D-12
10.	0.10795D-08	0.10470D-08	0.83402D-12
20.	0.10795D-08	0.95339D-09	0.83395D-12
30.	0.10793D-08	0.80991D-09	0.83382D-12
40.	0.10792D-08	0.63951D-09	0.83364D-12
45.	0.10791D-08	0.54025D-09	0.83353D-12
50.	0.10789D-08	0.44660D-09	0.83341D-12
60.	0.10787D-08	0.27059D-09	0.83314D-12
70.	0.10784D-08	0.12710D-09	0.83283D-12
80.	0.10781D-08	0.33421D-10	0.83249D-12
90.	0.10778D-08	0.83235D-12	0.83213D-12
100.	0.10776D-08	0.33224D-10	0.83174D-12
110.	0.10773D-08	0.12664D-09	0.83136D-12
120.	0.10770D-08	0.26976D-09	0.83099D-12
130.	0.10767D-08	0.44529D-09	0.83065D-12
135.	0.10766D-08	0.53867D-09	0.83049D-12
150.	0.10764D-08	0.80746D-09	0.83009D-12
165.	0.10762D-08	0.10042D-08	0.82983D-12
180.	0.10761D-08	0.10761D-08	0.82974D-12

ALPHA = 0.06

THETA	SS	PP	SP
0.	0.12304D-07	0.123C4D-07	0.95330D-11
5.	0.12304D-07	0.12211D-07	0.95328D-11
10.	0.12304D-07	0.11934D-07	0.95323D-11
20.	0.12302D-07	0.10867D-07	0.95303D-11
30.	0.12298D-07	0.92315D-08	0.95271D-11
40.	0.12294D-07	0.72257D-08	0.95225D-11
45.	0.12291D-07	0.61584D-08	0.95197D-11
50.	0.12289D-07	0.50911D-C8	0.95167D-11
60.	0.12282D-07	0.30852D-08	0.95098D-11
70.	0.12275D-07	0.14497D-08	0.95018D-11
80.	0.12268D-07	0.38180D-09	0.94931D-11
90.	0.12260D-07	0.94895D-11	0.94836D-11
100.	0.12253D-07	0.37673D-09	0.94739D-11
110.	0.12245D-07	0.14380D-C8	0.94641D-11
120.	0.12239D-07	0.30640D-C8	0.94546D-11
130.	0.12232D-07	0.50575D-C8	0.94458D-11
135.	0.12229D-07	0.61177D-08	0.94417D-11
150.	0.12223D-07	0.91686D-08	0.94315D-11
165.	0.12218D-07	0.11400D-07	0.94249D-11
180.	0.12217D-07	0.12217D-07	0.94226D-11

ALPHA = 0.08

THETA	SS	PP	SP
0.	0.69192D-07	0.69192D-07	0.53819D-10
5.	0.69191D-07	0.68667D-07	0.53818D-10
10.	0.69186D-07	0.67109D-07	0.53813D-10
20.	0.69166D-07	0.61109D-07	0.53793D-10
30.	0.69134D-07	0.51916D-07	0.53760D-10
40.	0.69090D-07	0.40639D-07	0.53714D-10
45.	0.69064D-07	0.34638D-07	0.53687D-10
50.	0.69036D-07	0.28637D-07	0.53657D-10
60.	0.68973D-07	0.17358D-07	0.53587D-10
70.	0.68904D-07	0.81615D-C8	0.53508D-10
80.	0.68831D-07	0.21539D-C8	0.53420D-10
90.	0.68755D-07	0.53385D-1C	0.53326D-10
100.	0.68679D-07	0.21033D-08	0.53229D-10
110.	0.68605D-C7	0.80439D-C8	0.53131D-10
120.	0.68536C-07	0.17146D-07	0.53036D-10
130.	0.68473D-07	0.28301D-07	0.52948D-10
135.	0.68445D-07	0.34232D-07	0.52907D-10
150.	0.68375D-07	0.51289D-07	0.52805D-10
165.	0.68332D-07	0.63757D-07	0.52739D-10
180.	0.68317D-07	0.68317D-07	0.52717D-10

ALPHA = 0.02

THETA	SS	PP	SP
0.	0.36295D-10	0.36295D-10	0.57819D-13
5.	0.36295D-10	0.36020D-10	0.57819D-13
10.	0.36295D-10	0.35203D-10	0.57819D-13
20.	0.36295D-10	0.32057D-10	0.57818D-13
30.	0.36293D-10	0.27236D-10	0.57817D-13
40.	0.36292D-10	0.21324D-10	0.57816D-13
45.	0.36291D-10	0.18177D-10	0.57815D-13
50.	0.36290D-10	0.15031D-10	0.57814D-13
60.	0.36288D-10	0.91181D-11	0.57812D-13
70.	0.36286D-10	0.42977D-11	0.57809D-13
80.	0.36283D-10	0.11511D-11	0.57806D-13
90.	0.36281D-10	0.57807D-13	0.57803D-13
100.	0.36278D-10	0.11492D-11	0.57799D-13
110.	0.36276D-10	0.42934D-11	0.57796D-13
120.	0.36274D-10	0.91106D-11	0.57792D-13
130.	0.36271D-10	0.15019D-10	0.57788D-13
135.	0.36270D-10	0.18163D-10	0.57787D-13
150.	0.36268D-10	0.27215D-10	0.57783D-13
165.	0.36267D-10	0.33841D-10	0.57780D-13
180.	0.36266D-10	0.36266D-10	0.57779D-13

ALPHA = 0.04

THETA	SS	PP	SP
0.	0.23245D-08	0.23245D-08	0.37067D-11
5.	0.23245D-08	0.23068D-08	0.37067D-11
10.	0.23244D-08	0.22545D-08	0.37066D-11
20.	0.23242D-08	0.20531D-08	0.37065D-11
30.	0.23240D-08	0.17444D-08	0.37062D-11
40.	0.23236D-08	0.13658D-08	0.37059D-11
45.	0.23234D-08	0.11643D-08	0.37057D-11
50.	0.23231D-08	0.96280D-09	0.37054D-11
60.	0.23226D-08	0.58412D-09	0.37049D-11
70.	0.23220D-08	0.27540D-09	0.37042D-11
80.	0.23214D-08	0.73844D-10	0.37034D-11
90.	0.23207D-08	0.37036D-11	0.37025D-11
100.	0.23201D-08	0.73359D-10	0.37016D-11
110.	0.23195D-08	0.27430D-09	0.37007D-11
120.	0.23189D-08	0.58220D-09	0.36997D-11
130.	0.23183D-08	0.95981D-09	0.36988D-11
135.	0.23181D-08	0.11607D-08	0.36984D-11
150.	0.23175D-08	0.17390D-08	0.36973D-11
165.	0.23171D-08	0.21621D-08	0.36966D-11
180.	0.23170D-08	0.23170D-08	0.36964D-11

P = 0.50   M = 1.30

ALPHA = 0.06

THETA	SS	PP	SP
0.	0.26507D-07	0.26507D-07	0.42340D-10
5.	0.26507D-07	0.26306D-07	0.42340D-10
10.	0.26506D-07	0.25709D-07	0.42339D-10
20.	0.26501D-07	0.23413D-07	0.42335D-10
30.	0.26494D-07	0.19894D-07	0.42329D-10
40.	0.26485D-07	0.15577D-07	0.42320D-10
45.	0.26479D-07	0.13279D-07	0.42314D-10
50.	0.26473D-07	0.10982D-07	0.42308D-10
60.	0.26459D-07	0.66643D-08	0.42294D-10
70.	0.26444D-07	0.31437D-08	0.42276D-10
80.	0.26428D-07	0.84440D-09	0.42256D-10
90.	0.26411D-07	0.42260D-10	0.42234D-10
100.	0.26395D-07	0.83196D-09	0.42211D-10
110.	0.26378D-07	0.31156D-08	0.42186D-10
120.	0.26363D-07	0.66149D-08	0.42162D-10
130.	0.26350D-07	0.10906D-07	0.42139D-10
135.	0.26343D-07	0.13188D-07	0.42128D-10
150.	0.26328D-07	0.19754D-07	0.42101D-10
165.	0.26319D-07	0.24558D-07	0.42083D-10
180.	0.26315D-07	0.26315D-07	0.42077D-10

ALPHA = 0.08

THETA	SS	PP	SP
0.	0.14917D-06	0.14917D-06	0.23883D-09
5.	0.14916D-06	0.14804D-06	0.23882D-09
10.	0.14915D-06	0.14468D-06	0.23882D-09
20.	0.14911D-06	0.13176D-06	0.23878D-09
30.	0.14904D-06	0.11196D-06	0.23872D-09
40.	0.14894D-06	0.87675D-07	0.23863D-09
45.	0.14889D-06	0.74751D-07	0.23857D-09
50.	0.14883D-06	0.61825D-07	0.23851D-09
60.	0.14869D-06	0.37529D-07	0.23836D-09
70.	0.14854D-06	0.17716D-07	0.23819D-09
80.	0.14838D-06	0.47700D-08	0.23799D-09
90.	0.14821D-06	0.23803D-09	0.23777D-09
100.	0.14804D-06	0.46458D-08	0.23754D-09
110.	0.14788D-06	0.17435D-07	0.23729D-09
120.	0.14773D-06	0.37035D-07	0.23705D-09
130.	0.14760D-06	0.61061D-07	0.23682D-09
135.	0.14753D-06	0.73834D-07	0.23671D-09
150.	0.14738D-06	0.11057D-06	0.23644D-09
165.	0.14729D-06	0.13743D-06	0.23626D-09
180.	0.14725D-06	0.14725D-06	0.23620D-09

P = 0.50   M = 1.40

ALPHA = 0.02

THETA	SS	PP	SP
0.	0.61546D-10	0.61546D-10	0.15965D-12
5.	0.61546D-10	0.61080D-10	0.15965D-12
10.	0.61546D-10	0.59695D-10	0.15965D-12
20.	0.61545D-10	0.54366D-10	0.15965D-12
30.	0.61543D-10	0.46200D-10	0.15964D-12
40.	0.61540D-10	0.36184D-10	0.15964D-12
45.	0.61539D-10	0.30854D-10	0.15964D-12
50.	0.61537D-10	0.25525D-10	0.15964D-12
60.	0.61533D-10	0.15508D-10	0.15963D-12
70.	0.61529D-10	0.73423D-11	0.15963D-12
80.	0.61525D-10	0.20119D-11	0.15962D-12
90.	0.61521D-10	0.15963D-12	0.15961D-12
100.	0.61516D-10	0.20083D-11	0.15961D-12
110.	0.61512D-10	0.73342D-11	0.15960D-12
120.	0.61508D-10	0.15494D-10	0.15959D-12
130.	0.61505D-10	0.25504D-10	0.15958D-12
135.	0.61503D-10	0.30830D-10	0.15958D-12
150.	0.61499D-10	0.46163D-10	0.15957D-12
165.	0.61497D-10	0.57388D-10	0.15956D-12
180.	0.61496D-10	0.61496D-10	0.15956D-12

ALPHA = 0.04

THETA	SS	PP	SP
0.	0.39428D-08	0.39428D-08	0.10237D-10
5.	0.39428D-08	0.39129D-08	0.10237D-10
10.	0.39427D-08	0.38243D-08	0.10237D-10
20.	0.39424D-08	0.34829D-08	0.10237D-10
30.	0.39419D-08	0.29599D-08	0.10237D-10
40.	0.39413D-08	0.23183D-08	0.10236D-10
45.	0.39409D-08	0.19769D-08	0.10236D-10
50.	0.39405D-08	0.16355D-08	0.10235D-10
60.	0.39396D-08	0.99388D-09	0.10234D-10
70.	0.39386D-08	0.47072D-09	0.10233D-10
80.	0.39375D-08	0.12914D-09	0.10231D-10
90.	0.39363D-08	0.10232D-10	0.10229D-10
100.	0.39352D-08	0.12821D-09	0.10227D-10
110.	0.39341D-08	0.46865D-09	0.10225D-10
120.	0.39331D-08	0.99033D-09	0.10223D-10
130.	0.39322D-08	0.16302D-08	0.10221D-10
135.	0.39318D-08	0.19706D-08	0.10220D-10
150.	0.39308D-08	0.29504D-08	0.10217D-10
165.	0.39301D-08	0.36675D-08	0.10216D-10
180.	0.39299D-08	0.39299D-08	0.10215D-10

ALPHA = 0.06

THETA	SS	PP	SP
0.	0.44984D-07	0.44984D-07	0.11699D-09
5.	0.44983D-07	0.44643D-07	0.11699D-09
10.	0.44982D-07	0.43632D-07	0.11699D-09
20.	0.44974D-07	0.39739D-07	0.11698D-09
30.	0.44962D-07	0.33774D-07	0.11697D-09
40.	0.44945D-07	0.26456D-07	0.11695D-09
45.	0.44936D-07	0.22561D-07	0.11694D-09
50.	0.44925D-07	0.18667D-07	0.11693D-09
60.	0.44901D-07	0.11347D-07	0.11690D-09
70.	0.44875D-07	0.53773D-08	0.11687D-09
80.	0.44847D-07	0.14781D-08	0.11682D-09
90.	0.44819D-07	0.11685D-09	0.11678D-09
100.	0.44790D-07	0.14542D-08	0.11673D-09
110.	0.44762D-07	0.53243D-08	0.11667D-09
120.	0.44736D-07	0.11256D-07	0.11662D-09
130.	0.44712D-07	0.18529D-07	0.11656D-09
135.	0.44702D-07	0.22398D-07	0.11654D-09
150.	0.44676D-07	0.33530D-07	0.11648D-09
165.	0.44659D-07	0.41674D-07	0.11643D-09
180.	0.44653D-07	0.44653D-07	0.11642D-09

ALPHA = 0.08

THETA	SS	PP	SP
0.	0.25332D-06	0.25332D-06	0.66030D-09
5.	0.25332D-06	0.25141D-06	0.66030D-09
10.	0.25330D-06	0.24571D-06	0.66028D-09
20.	0.25323D-06	0.22380D-06	0.66022D-09
30.	0.25310D-06	0.19022D-06	0.66010D-09
40.	0.25294D-06	0.14902D-06	0.65994D-09
45.	0.25284D-06	0.12710D-06	0.65983D-09
50.	0.25273D-06	0.10517D-06	0.65971D-09
60.	0.25250D-06	0.63954D-07	0.65942D-09
70.	0.25224D-06	0.30335D-07	0.65907D-09
80.	0.25196D-06	0.83612D-08	0.65865D-09
90.	0.25167D-06	0.65890D-09	0.65818D-09
100.	0.25139D-06	0.81221D-08	0.65767D-09
110.	0.25111D-06	0.29806D-07	0.65713D-09
120.	0.25085D-06	0.63047D-07	0.65658D-09
130.	0.25061D-06	0.10380D-06	0.65606D-09
135.	0.25051D-06	0.12547D-06	0.65581D-09
150.	0.25024D-06	0.18779D-06	0.65518D-09
165.	0.25008D-06	0.23336D-06	0.65477D-09
180.	0.25002D-06	0.25002D-06	0.65462D-09

ALPHA = 0.02

THETA	SS	PP	SP
0.	0.43726D-10	0.43726D-10	0.10682D-13
5.	0.43726D-10	0.43394D-10	0.10682D-13
10.	0.43725D-10	0.42409D-10	0.10683D-13
20.	0.43721D-10	0.38615D-10	0.10686D-13
30.	0.43714D-10	0.32801D-10	0.10691D-13
40.	0.43705D-10	0.25670D-10	0.10697D-13
45.	0.43700D-10	0.21875D-10	0.10701D-13
50.	0.43694D-10	0.18079D-10	0.10705D-13
60.	0.43681D-10	0.10946D-10	0.10714D-13
70.	0.43667D-10	0.51299D-11	0.10723D-13
80.	0.43652D-10	0.13325D-11	0.10733D-13
90.	0.43636D-10	0.10748D-13	0.10743D-13
100.	0.43620D-10	0.13222D-11	0.10752D-13
110.	0.43605D-10	0.51059D-11	0.10761D-13
120.	0.43591D-10	0.10903D-10	0.10768D-13
130.	0.43578D-10	0.18011D-10	0.10775D-13
135.	0.43572D-10	0.21791D-10	0.10778D-13
150.	0.43558D-10	0.32672D-10	0.10785D-13
165.	0.43549D-10	0.40633D-10	0.10790D-13
180.	0.43546D-10	0.43546D-10	0.10791D-13

ALPHA = 0.04

THETA	SS	PP	SP
0.	0.27944D-08	0.27944D-08	0.66786D-12
5.	0.27943D-08	0.27732D-08	0.66792D-12
10.	0.27940D-08	0.27103D-08	0.66811D-12
20.	0.27930D-08	0.24681D-08	0.66888D-12
30.	0.27913D-08	0.20970D-08	0.67011D-12
40.	0.27890D-08	0.16416D-08	0.67175D-12
45.	0.27876D-08	0.13991D-08	0.67271D-12
50.	0.27861D-08	0.11566D-08	0.67374D-12
60.	0.27828D-08	0.70074D-09	0.67598D-12
70.	0.27792D-08	0.32888D-09	0.67839D-12
80.	0.27753D-08	0.85841D-10	0.68088D-12
90.	0.27713D-08	0.68487D-12	0.68336D-12
100.	0.27673D-08	0.83191D-10	0.68574D-12
110.	0.27634D-08	0.32272D-09	0.68796D-12
120.	0.27598D-08	0.68961D-09	0.68997D-12
130.	0.27565D-08	0.11390D-08	0.69172D-12
135.	0.27550D-08	0.13778D-08	0.69249D-12
150.	0.27513D-08	0.20639D-08	0.69434D-12
165.	0.27490D-08	0.25651D-08	0.69546D-12
180.	0.27482D-08	0.27482D-08	0.69583D-12

ALPHA = 0.06

THETA	SS	PP	SP
0.	0.31751D-07	0.31751D-07	0.73075D-11
5.	0.31749D-07	0.31511D-07	0.73092D-11
10.	0.31742D-07	0.30798D-07	0.73141D-11
20.	0.31716D-07	0.28053D-07	0.73337D-11
30.	0.31672D-07	0.23843D-07	0.73652D-11
40.	0.31613D-07	0.18673D-07	0.74074D-11
45.	0.31578D-07	0.15921D-07	0.74319D-11
50.	0.31540D-07	0.13166D-07	0.74583D-11
60.	0.31456D-07	0.79857D-08	0.75158D-11
70.	0.31362D-07	0.37569D-08	0.75776D-11
80.	0.31263D-07	0.98843D-09	0.76413D-11
90.	0.31160D-07	0.77435D-11	0.77048D-11
100.	0.31057D-07	0.92050D-09	0.77658D-11
110.	0.30958D-07	0.35989D-08	0.78228D-11
120.	0.30864D-07	0.77004D-08	0.78743D-11
130.	0.30780D-07	0.12714D-07	0.79192D-11
135.	0.30742D-07	0.15373D-07	0.79389D-11
150.	0.30648D-07	0.22996D-07	0.79862D-11
165.	0.30589D-07	0.28544D-07	0.80149D-11
180.	0.30569D-07	0.30569D-07	0.80245D-11

ALPHA = 0.08

THETA	SS	PP	SP
0.	0.17778D-06	0.17778D-06	0.38700D-10
5.	0.17776D-06	0.17644D-06	0.38717D-10
10.	0.17769D-06	0.17246D-06	0.38766D-10
20.	0.17743D-06	0.15714D-06	0.38961D-10
30.	0.17699D-06	0.13362D-06	0.39277D-10
40.	0.17640D-06	0.10472D-06	0.39698D-10
45.	0.17605D-06	0.89325D-07	0.39943D-10
50.	0.17567D-06	0.73910D-07	0.40207D-10
60.	0.17483D-06	0.44898D-07	0.40781D-10
70.	0.17390D-06	0.21193D-07	0.41398D-10
80.	0.17290D-06	0.56374D-08	0.42035D-10
90.	0.17188D-06	0.43055D-10	0.42668D-10
100.	0.17085D-06	0.49588D-08	0.43278D-10
110.	0.16986D-06	0.19615D-07	0.43848D-10
120.	0.16893D-06	0.42049D-07	0.44362D-10
130.	0.16808D-06	0.69393D-07	0.44810D-10
135.	0.16770D-06	0.83855D-07	0.45007D-10
150.	0.16677D-06	0.12516D-06	0.45479D-10
165.	0.16618D-06	0.15509D-06	0.45766D-10
180.	0.16597D-06	0.16597D-06	0.45862D-10

ALPHA = 0.02

THETA	SS	PP	SP
0.	0.17244D-09	0.17244D-09	0.15888D-12
5.	0.17244D-09	0.17113D-09	0.15888D-12
10.	0.17243D-09	0.16725D-09	0.15889D-12
20.	0.17242D-09	0.15230D-09	0.15892D-12
30.	0.17239D-09	0.12939D-09	0.15898D-12
40.	0.17236D-09	0.10129D-09	0.15906D-12
45.	0.17234D-09	0.86335D-10	0.15911D-12
50.	0.17232D-09	0.71378D-10	0.15915D-12
60.	0.17227D-09	0.43265D-10	0.15926D-12
70.	0.17222D-09	0.20342D-10	0.15937D-12
80.	0.17216D-09	0.53725D-11	0.15949D-12
90.	0.17210D-09	0.15969D-12	0.15960D-12
100.	0.17205D-09	0.53255D-11	0.15971D-12
110.	0.17199D-09	0.20237D-10	0.15981D-12
120.	0.17194D-09	0.43085D-10	0.15990D-12
130.	0.17189D-09	0.71103D-10	0.15997D-12
135.	0.17187D-09	0.86007D-10	0.16001D-12
150.	0.17181D-09	0.12890D-09	0.16008D-12
165.	0.17178D-09	0.16029D-09	0.16013D-12
180.	0.17177D-09	0.17177D-09	0.16015D-12

ALPHA = 0.04

THETA	SS	PP	SP
0.	0.11021D-07	0.11021D-07	0.99757D-11
5.	0.11021D-07	0.10938D-07	0.99765D-11
10.	0.11020D-07	0.10690D-07	0.99788D-11
20.	0.11016D-07	0.97365D-08	0.99881D-11
30.	0.11010D-07	0.82746D-08	0.10003D-10
40.	0.11001D-07	0.64802D-08	0.10023D-10
45.	0.10996D-07	0.55249D-08	0.10035D-10
50.	0.10991D-07	0.45692D-08	0.10047D-10
60.	0.10979D-07	0.27721D-08	0.10074D-10
70.	0.10965D-07	0.13058D-08	0.10103D-10
80.	0.10951D-07	0.34681D-09	0.10132D-10
90.	0.10936D-07	0.10183D-10	0.10161D-10
100.	0.10921D-07	0.33478D-09	0.10189D-10
110.	0.10907D-07	0.12789D-08	0.10214D-10
120.	0.10893D-07	0.27259D-08	0.10237D-10
130.	0.10881D-07	0.44988D-08	0.10256D-10
135.	0.10875D-07	0.54410D-08	0.10265D-10
150.	0.10862D-07	0.81491D-08	0.10285D-10
165.	0.10853D-07	0.10127D-07	0.10297D-10
180.	0.10850D-07	0.10850D-07	0.10301D-10

ALPHA = 0.06

THETA	SS	PP	SP
0.	0.12526D-06	0.12526D-06	0.10998D-09
5.	0.12525D-06	0.12432D-06	0.11000D-09
10.	0.12523D-06	0.12151D-06	0.11006D-09
20.	0.12513D-06	0.11070D-06	0.11030D-09
30.	0.12497D-06	0.94129D-07	0.11068D-09
40.	0.12475D-06	0.73768D-07	0.11119D-09
45.	0.12462D-06	0.62922D-07	0.11149D-09
50.	0.12448D-06	0.52066D-07	0.11180D-09
60.	0.12417D-06	0.31637D-07	0.11249D-09
70.	0.12382D-06	0.14947D-07	0.11323D-09
80.	0.12345D-06	0.40068D-08	0.11398D-09
90.	0.12307D-06	0.11530D-09	0.11472D-09
100.	0.12269D-06	0.36984D-08	0.11543D-09
110.	0.12232D-06	0.14260D-07	0.11608D-09
120.	0.12197D-06	0.30453D-07	0.11667D-09
130.	0.12166D-06	0.50261D-07	0.11717D-09
135.	0.12152D-06	0.60771D-07	0.11739D-09
150.	0.12117D-06	0.90913D-07	0.11791D-09
165.	0.12095D-06	0.11286D-06	0.11822D-09
180.	0.12088D-06	0.12088D-06	0.11832D-09

ALPHA = 0.08

THETA	SS	PP	SP
0.	0.70161D-06	0.70161D-06	0.58919D-09
5.	0.70153D-06	0.69634D-06	0.58939D-09
10.	0.70128D-06	0.68070D-06	0.59000D-09
20.	0.70029D-06	0.62043D-06	0.59237D-09
30.	0.69867D-06	0.52791D-06	0.59621D-09
40.	0.69648D-06	0.41412D-06	0.60131D-09
45.	0.69519D-06	0.35345D-06	0.60427D-09
50.	0.69378D-06	0.29269D-06	0.60745D-09
60.	0.69066D-06	0.17823D-06	0.61434D-09
70.	0.68720D-06	0.84561D-07	0.62169D-09
80.	0.68351D-06	0.22957D-07	0.62920D-09
90.	0.67970D-06	0.64236D-09	0.63661D-09
100.	0.67590D-06	0.19876D-07	0.64368D-09
110.	0.67221D-06	0.77695D-07	0.65020D-09
120.	0.66875D-06	0.16640D-06	0.65601D-09
130.	0.66562D-06	0.27467D-06	0.66103D-09
135.	0.66421D-06	0.33198D-06	0.66321D-09
150.	0.66073D-06	0.49578D-06	0.66840D-09
165.	0.65854D-06	0.61456D-06	0.67151D-09
180.	0.65780D-06	0.65780D-06	0.67254D-09

ALPHA = 0.02

THETA	SS	PP	SP
0.	0.67301D-09	0.67301D-09	0.22004D-11
5.	0.67301D-09	0.66792D-09	0.22004D-11
10.	0.67299D-09	0.65280D-09	0.22005D-11
20.	0.67294D-09	0.59461D-09	0.22008D-11
30.	0.67285D-09	0.50543D-09	0.22013D-11
40.	0.67272D-09	0.39602D-09	0.22018D-11
45.	0.67265D-09	0.33779D-09	0.22022D-11
50.	0.67257D-09	0.27956D-09	0.22025D-11
60.	0.67240D-09	0.17009D-09	0.22033D-11
70.	0.67220D-09	0.80820D-10	0.22041D-11
80.	0.67200D-09	0.22518D-10	0.22048D-11
90.	0.67178D-09	0.22068D-11	0.22056D-11
100.	0.67157D-09	0.22312D-10	0.22062D-11
110.	0.67136D-09	0.80375D-10	0.22068D-11
120.	0.67117D-09	0.16935D-09	0.22072D-11
130.	0.67099D-09	0.27847D-09	0.22076D-11
135.	0.67091D-09	0.33652D-09	0.22077D-11
150.	0.67072D-09	0.50358D-09	0.22080D-11
165.	0.67060D-09	0.62582D-09	0.22082D-11
180.	0.67055D-09	0.67055D-09	0.22083D-11

ALPHA = 0.04

THETA	SS	PP	SP
0.	0.43045D-07	0.43045D-07	0.13933D-09
5.	0.43044D-07	0.42720D-07	0.13933D-09
10.	0.43040D-07	0.41756D-07	0.13935D-09
20.	0.43026D-07	0.38042D-07	0.13942D-09
30.	0.43003D-07	0.32349D-07	0.13954D-09
40.	0.42971D-07	0.25361D-07	0.13969D-09
45.	0.42953D-07	0.21639D-07	0.13978D-09
50.	0.42933D-07	0.17916D-07	0.13987D-09
60.	0.42888D-07	0.10913D-07	0.14006D-09
70.	0.42838D-07	0.51966D-08	0.14026D-09
80.	0.42785D-07	0.14563D-08	0.14046D-09
90.	0.42730D-07	0.14095D-09	0.14064D-09
100.	0.42676D-07	0.14035D-08	0.14081D-09
110.	0.42623D-07	0.50827D-08	0.14095D-09
120.	0.42573D-07	0.10724D-07	0.14107D-09
130.	0.42528D-07	0.17638D-07	0.14116D-09
135.	0.42508D-07	0.21313D-07	0.14120D-09
150.	0.42458D-07	0.31877D-07	0.14128D-09
165.	0.42426D-07	0.39594D-07	0.14132D-09
180.	0.42415D-07	0.42415D-07	0.14134D-09

ALPHA = 0.06

THETA	SS	PP	SP
0.	0.48978D-06	0.48978D-06	0.15585D-08
5.	0.48975D-06	0.48610D-06	0.15587D-08
10.	0.48966D-06	0.47517D-06	0.15592D-08
20.	0.48929D-06	0.43309D-06	0.15610D-08
30.	0.48870D-06	0.36852D-06	0.15640D-08
40.	0.48789D-06	0.28917D-06	0.15678D-08
45.	0.48742D-06	0.24688D-06	0.15701D-08
50.	0.48690D-06	0.20454D-06	0.15724D-08
60.	0.48575D-06	0.12483D-06	0.15774D-08
70.	0.48447D-06	0.59650D-07	0.15825D-08
80.	0.48311D-06	0.16875D-07	0.15875D-08
90.	0.48171D-06	0.16002D-08	0.15922D-08
100.	0.48031D-06	0.15523D-07	0.15965D-08
110.	0.47895D-06	0.56732D-07	0.16001D-08
120.	0.47768D-06	0.11959D-06	0.16031D-08
130.	0.47653D-06	0.19742D-06	0.16055D-08
135.	0.47601D-06	0.23851D-06	0.16065D-08
150.	0.47473D-06	0.35641D-06	0.16086D-08
165.	0.47392D-06	0.44230D-06	0.16097D-08
180.	0.47365D-06	0.47365D-06	0.16100D-08

ALPHA = 0.08

THETA	SS	PP	SP
0.	0.27477D-05	0.27477D-05	0.85328D-08
5.	0.27474D-05	0.27272D-05	0.85344D-08
10.	0.27465D-05	0.26663D-05	0.85391D-08
20.	0.27429D-05	0.24315D-05	0.85576D-08
30.	0.27370D-05	0.20709D-05	0.85871D-08
40.	0.27289D-05	0.16270D-05	0.86258D-08
45.	0.27241D-05	0.13902D-05	0.86478D-08
50.	0.27190D-05	0.11529D-05	0.86713D-08
60.	0.27075D-05	0.70544D-06	0.87210D-08
70.	0.26947D-05	0.33876D-06	0.87721D-08
80.	0.26812D-05	0.97067D-07	0.88223D-08
90.	0.26672D-05	0.89488D-08	0.88694D-08
100.	0.26532D-05	0.83565D-07	0.89116D-08
110.	0.26396D-05	0.30961D-06	0.89480D-08
120.	0.26269D-05	0.65711D-06	0.89781D-08
130.	0.26154D-05	0.10817D-05	0.90019D-08
135.	0.26102D-05	0.13066D-05	0.90115D-08
150.	0.25974D-05	0.19499D-05	0.90325D-08
165.	0.25893D-05	0.24166D-05	0.90437D-08
180.	0.25866D-05	0.25866D-05	0.90471D-08

P = 0.20   M = 1.30

ALPHA = 0.02

THETA	SS	PP	SP
0.	0.14828D-08	0.14828D-08	0.96583D-11
5.	0.14828D-08	0.14716D-08	0.96584D-11
10.	0.14828D-08	0.14384D-08	0.96586D-11
20.	0.14827D-08	0.13107D-08	0.96593D-11
30.	0.14825D-08	0.11148D-08	0.96605D-11
40.	0.14822D-08	0.87457D-09	0.96619D-11
45.	0.14821D-08	0.74670D-09	0.96627D-11
50.	0.14819D-08	0.61882D-09	0.96636D-11
60.	0.14815D-08	0.37841D-09	0.96653D-11
70.	0.14811D-08	0.18236D-09	0.96670D-11
80.	0.14806D-08	0.54301D-10	0.96684D-11
90.	0.14802D-08	0.96749D-11	0.96696D-11
100.	0.14797D-08	0.53816D-10	0.96705D-11
110.	0.14793D-08	0.18133D-09	0.96710D-11
120.	0.14789D-08	0.37674D-09	0.96713D-11
130.	0.14785D-08	0.61640D-09	0.96713D-11
135.	0.14783D-08	0.74389D-09	0.96712D-11
150.	0.14779D-08	0.11108D-08	0.96708D-11
165.	0.14777D-08	0.13793D-08	0.96704D-11
180.	0.14776D-08	0.14776D-08	0.96703D-11

ALPHA = 0.04

THETA	SS	PP	SP
0.	0.94921D-07	0.94921D-07	0.61466D-09
5.	0.94918D-07	0.94207D-07	0.61467D-09
10.	0.94910D-07	0.92088D-07	0.61472D-09
20.	0.94880D-07	0.83930D-07	0.61491D-09
30.	0.94831D-07	0.71422D-07	0.61520D-09
40.	0.94763D-07	0.56065D-07	0.61557D-09
45.	0.94724D-07	0.47887D-07	0.61578D-09
50.	0.94680D-07	0.39704D-07	0.61600D-09
60.	0.94584D-07	0.24310D-07	0.61644D-09
70.	0.94478D-07	0.11741D-07	0.61686D-09
80.	0.94365D-07	0.35150D-08	0.61724D-09
90.	0.94248D-07	0.61850D-09	0.61754D-09
100.	0.94131D-07	0.33909D-08	0.61777D-09
110.	0.94018D-07	0.11478D-07	0.61791D-09
120.	0.93912D-07	0.23881D-07	0.61797D-09
130.	0.93816D-07	0.39084D-07	0.61796D-09
135.	0.93773D-07	0.47165D-07	0.61794D-09
150.	0.93666D-07	0.70398D-07	0.61785D-09
165.	0.93599D-07	0.87371D-07	0.61775D-09
180.	0.93576D-07	0.93576D-07	0.61771D-09

ALPHA = 0.06

THETA	SS	PP	SP
0.	0.10816D-05	0.10816D-05	0.69353D-08
5.	0.10815D-05	0.10735D-05	0.69357D-08
10.	0.10813D-05	0.1C495D-05	0.69369D-08
20.	0.10806D-05	0.95693D-06	0.69417D-08
30.	0.10793D-05	0.81493D-06	0.69492D-08
40.	0.10776D-05	C.64036D-06	0.69588D-08
45.	0.10765D-05	0.54731D-06	0.69642D-08
50.	0.10754D-05	0.45413D-06	0.69697D-08
60.	0.10730D-05	0.27864D-06	0.69810D-08
70.	0.10703D-05	0.1350CD-06	0.69918D-08
80.	0.10673D-C5	0.40793D-07	0.70014D-08
90.	0.10644D-05	0.70441D-08	0.70093D-08
100.	0.10614D-05	0.37613D-07	0.70150D-08
110.	0.10585D-C5	0.12832D-06	0.70186D-08
120.	0.10557D-05	0.26765D-06	0.70201D-08
130.	0.10533D-C5	0.43826D-C6	0.70200D-08
135.	0.10522D-05	0.52882D-06	0.70195D-08
150.	0.10494D-05	0.78868D-06	0.70170D-08
165.	0.10477D-05	0.978C1D-06	0.70146D-08
180.	0.10471D-05	0.10471D-05	0.70136D-08

ALPHA = 0.08

THETA	SS	PP	SP
0.	0.60801D-05	0.608C1D-05	0.38448D-07
5.	0.60794D-05	0.60350D-C5	0.38452D-07
10.	0.60775D-05	C.590C8D-C5	0.38464D-07
20.	0.60697D-05	0.53839D-05	0.38512D-07
30.	0.60570D-05	0.45897D-05	0.38587D-07
40.	0.60398D-05	0.36118C-C5	0.38683D-07
45.	0.60297D-05	0.30897D-C5	0.38736D-07
50.	0.60186D-05	0.25664D-C5	0.38791D-07
60.	0.59940D-05	0.15793D-C5	0.38904D-07
70.	0.59668D-05	0.76954D-06	0.39012D-07
80.	0.59378D-05	0.23514D-C6	0.39108D-07
90.	0.59079D-05	0.39534D-C7	0.39186D-07
100.	0.58781D-05	0.20337D-06	0.39244D-07
110.	0.58491D-05	0.702C2D-06	0.39279D-07
120.	0.58219D-05	0.14695D-05	0.39295D-07
130.	0.57973D-05	C.24079D-C5	0.39294D-07
135.	0.57862D-05	0.29051D-C5	0.39289D-07
150.	0.57589D-C5	0.43275D-C5	0.39264D-07
165.	0.57417D-05	0.53598D-05	0.39240D-07
180.	0.57358D-C5	0.57358D-C5	0.39230D-07

ALPHA = 0.02

THETA	SS	PP	SP
0.	0.25869D-08	0.25869D-08	0.26530D-10
5.	0.25869D-08	0.25675D-08	0.26530D-10
10.	0.25869D-08	0.25098D-08	0.26531D-10
20.	0.25867D-08	0.22877D-08	0.26532D-10
30.	0.25863D-08	0.19474D-08	0.26533D-10
40.	0.25859D-08	0.15299D-08	0.26536D-10
45.	0.25856D-08	0.13076D-08	0.26537D-10
50.	0.25853D-08	0.10854D-08	0.26538D-10
60.	0.25847D-08	0.66751D-09	0.26540D-10
70.	0.25840D-08	0.32674D-09	0.26541D-10
80.	0.25832D-08	0.10415D-09	0.26542D-10
90.	0.25824D-08	0.26557D-10	0.26542D-10
100.	0.25816D-08	0.10326D-09	0.26541D-10
110.	0.25809D-08	0.32487D-09	0.26540D-10
120.	0.25802D-08	0.66451D-09	0.26537D-10
130.	0.25795D-08	0.10811D-08	0.26535D-10
135.	0.25792D-08	0.13027D-08	0.26533D-10
150.	0.25785D-08	0.19405D-08	0.26529D-10
165.	0.25781D-08	0.24072D-08	0.26526D-10
180.	0.25779D-08	0.25779D-08	0.26525D-10

ALPHA = 0.04

THETA	SS	PP	SP
0.	0.16576D-06	0.16576D-06	0.16945D-08
5.	0.16575D-06	0.16451D-06	0.16945D-08
10.	0.16574D-06	0.16083D-06	0.16946D-08
20.	0.16569D-06	0.14664D-06	0.16949D-08
30.	0.16560D-06	0.12489D-06	0.16953D-08
40.	0.16549D-06	0.98178D-07	0.16959D-08
45.	0.16542D-06	0.83952D-07	0.16962D-08
50.	0.16534D-06	0.69717D-07	0.16964D-08
60.	0.16518D-06	0.42936D-07	0.16970D-08
70.	0.16500D-06	0.21066D-07	0.16974D-08
80.	0.16480D-06	0.67469D-08	0.16976D-08
90.	0.16460D-06	0.17013D-08	0.16976D-08
100.	0.16440D-06	0.65187D-08	0.16974D-08
110.	0.16421D-06	0.20586D-07	0.16969D-08
120.	0.16403D-06	0.42166D-07	0.16963D-08
130.	0.16386D-06	0.68621D-07	0.16956D-08
135.	0.16379D-06	0.82683D-07	0.16953D-08
150.	0.16360D-06	0.12311D-06	0.16942D-08
165.	0.16349D-06	0.15265D-06	0.16935D-08
180.	0.16345D-06	0.16345D-06	0.16932D-08

ALPHA = 0.06

THETA	SS	PP	SP
0.	0.18917D-05	0.18917D-05	0.19236D-07
5.	0.18916D-05	0.18776D-05	0.19237D-07
10.	0.18912D-05	0.18358D-C5	0.19239D-07
20.	0.18899D-05	0.16747D-05	0.19246D-07
30.	0.18877D-05	0.14274D-05	0.19258D-07
40.	0.18848D-05	0.11234D-05	0.19272D-07
45.	0.18830D-05	0.96129D-06	0.19279D-07
50.	0.18811D-05	0.79896D-06	0.19286D-07
60.	0.18769D-05	0.49314D-06	0.19300D-07
70.	0.18722D-05	0.24288D-06	0.19310D-07
80.	0.18673D-05	0.78358D-07	0.19315D-07
90.	0.18621D-05	0.19411D-07	0.19315D-07
100.	0.18570D-05	0.72548D-07	0.19309D-07
110.	0.18520D-05	0.23058D-06	0.19298D-07
120.	0.18474D-05	0.47342D-06	0.19283D-07
130.	0.18431D-05	0.77085D-06	0.19265D-07
135.	0.18412D-05	0.92876D-06	0.19256D-07
150.	0.18365D-05	0.13819D-C5	0.19229D-07
165.	0.18336D-05	0.17121D-05	0.19210D-07
180.	0.18326D-05	0.18326D-05	0.19203D-07

ALPHA = 0.08

THETA	SS	PP	SP
0.	0.10657D-C4	0.10657D-04	0.10757D-06
5.	0.10656D-C4	0.10579D-04	0.10757D-06
10.	0.10653D-C4	0.10345D-04	0.10759D-06
20.	0.10640D-04	0.94433D-C5	0.10767D-06
30.	0.10618D-04	0.80581D-05	0.10778D-06
40.	0.10588D-C4	0.63518D-05	0.10792D-06
45.	0.10571D-C4	0.54407D-C4	0.10800D-06
50.	0.10552D-C4	0.45271D-05	0.10807D-06
60.	0.10510D-C4	0.28029D-C5	0.10820D-06
70.	0.10463D-04	0.13877D-05	0.10830D-06
80.	0.10413D-C4	0.45266D-06	0.10836D-06
90.	0.10362D-04	0.10931D-06	0.10836D-06
100.	0.10311D-04	0.39423D-C6	0.10830D-06
110.	0.10261D-04	0.12648D-05	0.10819D-06
120.	0.10215D-04	0.26059D-C5	0.10804D-06
130.	0.10172D-C4	0.42464D-05	0.10786D-06
135.	0.10153D-04	0.51158D-C5	0.10777D-06
150.	0.10107D-C4	0.76035D-05	0.10750D-06
165.	0.10077D-04	0.94093D-C5	0.10731D-06
180.	0.10C67D-04	0.10067D-04	0.10724D-06

P = 0.10   M = 1.05

ALPHA = 0.02

THETA	SS	PP	SP
0.	0.69866D-09	0.69866D-09	0.25712D-12
5.	0.69864D-09	0.69337D-09	0.25717D-12
10.	0.69859D-09	0.67767D-09	0.25733D-12
20.	0.69836D-09	0.61721D-09	0.25794D-12
30.	0.69798D-09	0.52453D-09	0.25893D-12
40.	0.69747D-09	0.41075D-09	0.26026D-12
45.	0.69717D-09	0.35017D-09	0.26104D-12
50.	0.69684D-09	0.28956D-09	0.26189D-12
60.	0.69612D-09	0.17557D-09	0.26375D-12
70.	0.69531D-09	0.82529D-10	0.26579D-12
80.	0.69446D-09	0.21662D-10	0.26792D-12
90.	0.69357D-09	0.27070D-12	0.27008D-12
100.	0.69269D-09	0.20840D-10	0.27220D-12
110.	0.69183D-09	0.80742D-10	0.27423D-12
120.	0.69103D-09	0.17258D-09	0.27610D-12
130.	0.69030D-09	0.28513D-09	0.27776D-12
135.	0.68997D-09	0.34495D-09	0.27850D-12
150.	0.68917D-09	0.51693D-09	0.28030D-12
165.	0.68866D-09	0.64256D-09	0.28142D-12
180.	0.68848D-09	0.68848D-09	0.28180D-12

ALPHA = 0.04

THETA	SS	PP	SP
0.	0.44306D-07	0.44306D-07	0.13462D-10
5.	0.44301D-07	0.43974D-07	0.13476D-10
10.	0.44286D-07	0.42988D-07	0.13515D-10
20.	0.44228D-07	0.39188D-07	0.13671D-10
30.	0.44132D-07	0.33352D-07	0.13925D-10
40.	0.44001D-07	0.26172D-07	0.14267D-10
45.	0.43925D-07	0.22341D-07	0.14467D-10
50.	0.43841D-07	0.18503D-07	0.14684D-10
60.	0.43655D-07	0.11268D-07	0.15161D-10
70.	0.43449D-07	0.53416D-08	0.15681D-10
80.	0.43230D-07	0.14375D-08	0.16226D-10
90.	0.43003D-07	0.16938D-10	0.16780D-10
100.	0.42777D-07	0.12270D-08	0.17324D-10
110.	0.42558D-07	0.48843D-08	0.17842D-10
120.	0.42352D-07	0.10504D-07	0.18320D-10
130.	0.42166D-07	0.17370D-07	0.18745D-10
135.	0.42082D-07	0.21006D-07	0.18935D-10
150.	0.41875D-07	0.31407D-07	0.19397D-10
165.	0.41745D-07	0.38953D-07	0.19684D-10
180.	0.41701D-07	0.41701D-07	0.19781D-10

ALPHA = 0.06

THETA	SS	PP	SP
0.	0.49692D-06	0.49692D-06	0.96518D-10
5.	0.49680D-06	0.49326D-06	0.96857D-10
10.	0.49642D-06	0.48239D-06	0.97871D-10
20.	0.49491D-06	0.44042D-06	0.10188D-09
30.	0.49245D-06	0.37577D-06	0.10838D-09
40.	0.48911D-06	0.29590D-06	0.11713D-09
45.	0.48715D-06	0.25315D-06	0.12226D-09
50.	0.48500D-06	0.21021D-06	0.12782D-09
60.	0.48023D-06	0.12896D-06	0.14004D-09
70.	0.47496D-06	0.61978D-07	0.15337D-09
80.	0.46933D-06	0.17345D-07	0.16736D-09
90.	0.46354D-06	0.18559D-09	0.18154D-09
100.	0.45774D-06	0.11950D-07	0.19548D-09
110.	0.45212D-06	0.50259D-07	0.20876D-09
120.	0.44684D-06	0.10937D-06	0.22101D-09
130.	0.44207D-06	0.18118D-06	0.23191D-09
135.	0.43993D-06	0.21895D-06	0.23677D-09
150.	0.43462D-06	0.32591D-06	0.24862D-09
165.	0.43128D-06	0.40248D-06	0.25597D-09
180.	0.43015D-06	0.43015D-06	0.25846D-09

ALPHA = 0.08

THETA	SS	PP	SP
0.	0.27311D-05	0.27311D-05	0.95296D-10
5.	0.27298D-05	0.27115D-05	0.98681D-10
10.	0.27260D-05	0.26532D-05	0.10880D-09
20.	0.27110D-05	0.24277D-05	0.14880D-09
30.	0.26864D-05	0.20788D-05	0.21377D-09
40.	0.26531D-05	0.16452D-05	0.30123D-09
45.	0.26334D-05	0.14119D-05	0.35241D-09
50.	0.26120D-05	0.11768D-05	0.40794D-09
60.	0.25643D-05	0.72931D-06	0.53003D-09
70.	0.25116D-05	0.35715D-06	0.66318D-09
80.	0.24555D-05	0.10509D-06	0.80287D-09
90.	0.23976D-05	0.98498D-09	0.94454D-09
100.	0.23397D-05	0.51202D-07	0.10838D-08
110.	0.22835D-05	0.24009D-06	0.12164D-08
120.	0.22308D-05	0.53372D-06	0.13388D-08
130.	0.21832D-05	0.88677D-06	0.14477D-08
135.	0.21617D-05	0.10703D-05	0.14962D-08
150.	0.21087D-05	0.15808D-05	0.16146D-08
165.	0.20754D-05	0.19372D-05	0.16880D-08
180.	0.20641D-05	0.20641D-05	0.17129D-08

ALPHA = 0.02

THETA	SS	PP	SP
0.	0.27643D-08	0.27643D-08	0.38877D-11
5.	0.27643D-08	0.27435D-08	0.38881D-11
10.	0.27641D-08	0.26814D-08	0.38893D-11
20.	0.27632D-08	0.24426D-08	0.38941D-11
30.	0.27618D-08	0.20764D-08	0.39018D-11
40.	0.27599D-08	0.16268D-08	0.39120D-11
45.	0.27587D-08	0.13874D-08	0.39180D-11
50.	0.27575D-08	0.11478D-08	0.39245D-11
60.	0.27548D-08	0.69724D-09	0.39385D-11
70.	0.27518D-08	0.32939D-09	0.39537D-11
80.	0.27485D-08	0.88671D-10	0.39693D-11
90.	0.27452D-08	0.39939D-11	0.39848D-11
100.	0.27419D-08	0.85242D-10	0.39999D-11
110.	0.27387D-08	0.32207D-09	0.40139D-11
120.	0.27356D-08	0.68527D-09	0.40266D-11
130.	0.27329D-08	0.11304D-08	0.40377D-11
135.	0.27317D-08	0.13671D-08	0.40425D-11
150.	0.27286D-08	0.20474D-08	0.40543D-11
165.	0.27267D-08	0.25444D-08	0.40614D-11
180.	0.27261D-08	0.27261D-08	0.40638D-11

ALPHA = 0.04

THETA	SS	PP	SP
0.	0.17533D-06	0.17533D-06	0.22315D-09
5.	0.17532D-06	0.17403D-06	0.22326D-09
10.	0.17526D-06	0.17013D-06	0.22356D-09
20.	0.17504D-06	0.15514D-06	0.22478D-09
30.	0.17468D-06	0.13210D-06	0.22675D-09
40.	0.17419D-06	0.10375D-06 ·	0.22939D-09
45.	0.17390D-06	0.88610D-07	0.23092D-09
50.	0.17359D-06	0.73441D-07	0.23257D-09
60.	0.17289D-06	0.44830D-07	0.23617D-09
70.	0.17211D-06	0.21371D-07	0.24004D-09
80.	0.17129D-06	0.58990D-08	0.24404D-09
90.	0.17044D-06	0.25035D-09	0.24802D-09
100.	0.16959D-06	0.50212D-08	0.25187D-09
110.	0.16876D-06	0.19497D-07	0.25546D-09
120.	0.16799D-06	0.41765D-07	0.25871D-09
130.	0.16729D-06	0.68988D-07	0.26155D-09
135.	0.16697D-06	0.83411D-07	0.26280D-09
150.	0.16619D-06	0.12468D-06	0.26580D-09
165.	0.16571D-06	0.15463D-06	0.26762D-09
180.	0.16554D-06	0.16554D-06	0.26823D-09

ALPHA = 0.06

THETA	SS	PP	SP
0.	0.19671D-05	0.19671D-05	0.20547D-08
5.	0.19666D-05	0.19527D-05	0.20574D-08
10.	0.19652D-05	0.19059D-05	0.20653D-08
20.	0.19596D-05	0.17446D-05	0.20965D-08
30.	0.19503D-05	0.14899D-05	0.21470D-08
40.	0.19378D-05	0.11747D-05	0.22145D-08
45.	0.19304D-05	0.10059D-05	0.22538D-08
50.	0.19223D-05	0.83615D-06	0.22961D-08
60.	0.19044D-05	0.51455D-06	0.23883D-08
70.	0.18845D-05	0.24893D-06	0.24875D-08
80.	0.18634D-05	0.71447D-07	0.25900D-08
90.	0.18416D-05	0.27518D-08	0.26921D-08
100.	0.18198D-05	0.48951D-07	0.27906D-08
110.	0.17987D-05	0.20090D-06	0.28827D-08
120.	0.17788D-05	0.43601D-06	0.29660D-08
130.	0.17609D-05	0.72203D-06	0.30388D-08
135.	0.17528D-05	0.87265D-06	0.30707D-08
150.	0.17329D-05	0.12995D-05	0.31476D-08
165.	0.17203D-05	0.16055D-05	0.31944D-08
180.	0.17161D-05	0.17161D-05	0.32101D-08

ALPHA = 0.08

THETA	SS	PP	SP
0.	0.10816D-04	0.10816D-04	0.77127D-08
5.	0.10811D-04	0.10739D-04	0.77392D-08
10.	0.10797D-04	0.10511D-04	0.78184D-08
20.	0.10741D-04	0.96255D-05	0.81305D-08
30.	0.10648D-04	0.82539D-05	0.86349D-08
40.	0.10523D-04	0.65455D-05	0.93092D-08
45.	0.10449D-04	0.56246D-05	0.97010D-08
50.	0.10368D-04	0.46951D-05	0.10124D-07
60.	0.10189D-04	0.29219D-05	0.11045D-07
70.	0.99911D-05	0.14420D-05	0.12036D-07
80.	0.97800D-05	0.43450D-06	0.13059D-07
90.	0.95623D-05	0.14676D-07	0.14079D-07
100.	0.93445D-05	0.21019D-06	0.15064D-07
110.	0.91334D-05	0.96220D-06	0.15983D-07
120.	0.89353D-05	0.21373D-05	0.16816D-07
130.	0.87563D-05	0.35551D-05	0.17542D-07
135.	0.86756D-05	0.42938D-05	0.17862D-07
150.	0.84763D-05	0.63530D-05	0.18630D-07
165.	0.83511D-05	0.77947D-05	0.19097D-07
180.	0.83083D-05	0.83083D-05	0.19254D-07

P = 0.10   M = 1.20

ALPHA = 0.02

THETA	SS	PP	SP
0.	0.10917D-07	0.10917D-07	0.54121D-10
5.	0.10917D-07	0.10835D-07	0.54123D-10
10.	0.10916D-07	0.10591D-07	0.54131D-10
20.	0.10913D-07	0.96515D-08	0.54160D-10
30.	0.10908D-07	0.82110D-08	0.54206D-10
40.	0.10900D-07	0.64422D-08	0.54267D-10
45.	0.10896D-07	0.55002D-08	0.54302D-10
50.	0.10892D-07	0.45576D-08	0.54339D-10
60.	0.10881D-07	0.27843D-08	0.54417D-10
70.	0.10870D-07	0.13363D-08	0.54497D-10
80.	0.10858D-07	0.38843D-09	0.54576D-10
90.	0.10846D-07	0.54775D-10	0.54650D-10
100.	0.10833D-07	0.37444D-09	0.54717D-10
110.	0.10821D-07	0.13068D-08	0.54774D-10
120.	0.10810D-07	0.27370D-08	0.54822D-10
130.	0.10800D-07	0.44901D-08	0.54859D-10
135.	0.10795D-07	0.54220D-08	0.54875D-10
150.	0.10784D-07	0.81013D-08	0.54908D-10
165.	0.10777D-07	0.10059D-07	0.54925D-10
180.	0.10774D-07	0.10774D-07	0.54931D-10

ALPHA = 0.04

THETA	SS	PP	SP
0.	0.69341D-06	0.69341D-06	0.32779D-08
5.	0.69334D-06	0.68826D-06	0.32785D-08
10.	0.69313D-06	0.67296D-06	0.32804D-08
20.	0.69231D-06	0.61358D-06	0.32879D-08
30.	0.69096D-06	0.52334D-06	0.32997D-08
40.	0.68914D-06	0.41170D-06	0.33153D-08
45.	0.68806D-06	0.35208D-06	0.33242D-08
50.	0.68689D-06	0.29231D-06	0.33336D-08
60.	0.68428D-06	0.17951D-06	0.33536D-08
70.	0.68140D-06	0.86936D-07	0.33743D-08
80.	0.67832D-06	0.25815D-07	0.33945D-08
90.	0.67515D-06	0.34454D-08	0.34135D-08
100.	0.67198D-06	0.22233D-07	0.34305D-08
110.	0.66891D-06	0.79396D-07	0.34452D-08
120.	0.66602D-06	0.16740D-06	0.34573D-08
130.	0.66342D-06	0.27502D-06	0.34669D-08
135.	0.66224D-06	0.33206D-06	0.34708D-08
150.	0.65934D-06	0.49527D-06	0.34793D-08
165.	0.65752D-06	0.61375D-06	0.34838D-08
180.	0.65690D-06	0.65690D-06	0.34852D-08

ALPHA = 0.06

THETA	SS	PP	SP
0.	0.77980D-05	0.77980D-05	0.33808D-07
5.	0.77962D-05	C.77414D-05	0.33825D-07
10.	0.77909D-05	0.75731D-05	0.33873D-07
20.	0.77698D-05	0.69231D-05	0.34064D-07
30.	0.77353D-05	0.59202D-05	0.34369D-07
40.	0.76885D-05	0.46781D-05	0.34768D-07
45.	0.76610D-05	0.40118D-05	0.34996D-07
50.	0.76309D-05	0.33415D-05	0.35238D-07
60.	0.75641D-05	0.20696D-05	0.35751D-07
70.	0.74901D-05	0.10171D-05	0.36279D-07
80.	0.74114D-05	0.31219D-06	0.36798D-07
90.	0.73301D-05	0.38102D-07	0.37284D-07
100.	0.72489D-05	0.22040D-06	0.37720D-07
110.	0.71701D-05	0.82384D-06	0.38097D-07
120.	0.70962D-05	0.17592D-05	0.38408D-07
130.	0.70294D-05	0.28983D-05	0.38654D-07
135.	0.69993D-05	0.34985D-05	0.38754D-07
150.	0.69249D-05	0.52007D-05	0.38972D-07
165.	0.68782D-05	0.64211D-05	0.39087D-07
180.	0.68622D-05	0.68622D-05	0.39123D-07

ALPHA = 0.08

THETA	SS	PP	SP
0.	0.43025D-04	C.43025D-04	0.16220D-06
5.	0.43007D-04	0.42723D-04	0.16237D-06
10.	0.42954D-04	0.41824D-04	0.16285D-06
20.	0.42743D-04	0.38343D-04	0.16476D-06
30.	0.42399D-04	0.32940D-04	0.16780D-06
40.	0.41931D-04	0.26195D-04	0.17179D-06
45.	0.41656D-04	0.22551D-04	0.17406D-06
50.	0.41355D-04	0.18868D-04	0.17648D-06
60.	0.40688D-04	0.11824D-04	0.18160D-06
70.	0.39950D-04	0.59258D-05	0.18688D-06
80.	0.39163D-04	0.18968D-05	0.19206D-06
90.	0.38351D-04	0.20509D-06	0.19692D-06
100.	0.37540D-04	0.97995D-06	0.20128D-06
110.	0.36753D-04	0.39954D-05	0.20504D-06
120.	0.36015D-04	0.87235D-05	0.20815D-06
130.	0.35347D-04	0.14441D-04	0.21060D-06
135.	0.35047D-04	0.17425D-04	0.21160D-06
150.	0.34304D-04	0.25754D-04	0.21378D-06
165.	0.33837D-04	0.31595D-04	0.21493D-06
180.	0.33678D-04	0.33678D-04	0.21529D-06

ALPHA = 0.02

THETA	SS	PP	SP
0.	0.24462D-07	0.24462D-07	0.23840D-09
5.	0.24462D-07	0.24279D-07	0.23840D-09
10.	0.24460D-07	0.23735D-07	0.23842D-09
20.	0.24453D-07	0.21641D-07	0.23849D-09
30.	0.24442D-07	0.18430D-07	0.23860D-09
40.	0.24427D-07	0.14486D-07	0.23873D-09
45.	0.24417D-07	0.12386D-07	0.23881D-09
50.	0.24408D-07	0.10284D-07	0.23888D-09
60.	0.24386D-07	0.63291D-08	0.23904D-09
70.	0.24361D-07	0.30993D-08	0.23918D-09
80.	0.24336D-07	0.98466D-09	0.23931D-09
90.	0.24309D-07	0.23995D-09	0.23941D-09
100.	0.24282D-07	0.95269D-09	0.23947D-09
110.	0.24256D-07	0.30325D-08	0.23950D-09
120.	0.24232D-07	0.62231D-08	0.23950D-09
130.	0.24210D-07	0.10134D-07	0.23948D-09
135.	0.24200D-07	0.12214D-07	0.23946D-09
150.	0.24176D-07	0.18191D-07	0.23940D-09
165.	0.24161D-07	0.22559D-07	0.23935D-09
180.	0.24155D-07	0.24155D-07	0.23933D-09

ALPHA = 0.04

THETA	SS	PP	SP
0.	0.15566D-05	0.15566D-05	0.14746D-07
5.	0.15564D-05	0.15451D-05	0.14747D-07
10.	0.15560D-05	0.15110D-05	0.14752D-07
20.	0.15542D-05	0.13794D-05	0.14769D-07
30.	0.15513D-05	0.11771D-05	0.14796D-07
40.	0.15474D-05	0.92789D-06	0.14831D-07
45.	0.15451D-05	0.79474D-06	0.14850D-07
50.	0.15426D-05	0.66121D-06	0.14870D-07
60.	0.15369D-05	0.40910D-06	0.14910D-07
70.	0.15307D-05	0.20208D-06	0.14947D-07
80.	0.15241D-05	0.65289D-07	0.14979D-07
90.	0.15173D-05	0.15144D-07	0.15004D-07
100.	0.15105D-05	0.57102D-07	0.15021D-07
110.	0.15038D-05	0.18499D-06	0.15028D-07
120.	0.14976D-05	0.38196D-06	0.15029D-07
130.	0.14920D-05	0.62292D-06	0.15023D-07
135.	0.14895D-05	0.75063D-06	0.15018D-07
150.	0.14833D-05	0.11161D-05	0.15002D-07
165.	0.14793D-05	0.13814D-05	0.14989D-07
180.	0.14780D-05	0.14780D-05	0.14983D-07

ALPHA = 0.06

THETA	SS	PP	SP
0.	0.17560D-04	0.17560D-04	0.15825D-06
5.	0.17556D-04	0.17433D-04	0.15829D-06
10.	0.17544D-04	0.17057D-04	0.15840D-06
20.	0.17499D-04	0.15605D-04	0.15885D-06
30.	0.17425D-04	0.13363D-04	0.15955D-06
40.	0.17324D-04	0.10584D-04	0.16044D-06
45.	0.17265D-04	0.90915D-05	0.16093D-06
50.	0.17200D-04	0.75894D-05	0.16144D-06
60.	0.17056D-04	0.47365D-05	0.16245D-06
70.	0.16897D-04	0.23725D-05	0.16341D-06
80.	0.16727D-04	0.78679D-06	0.16424D-06
90.	0.16552D-04	0.16845D-06	0.16487D-06
100.	0.16378D-04	0.57697D-06	0.16529D-06
110.	0.16208D-04	0.19345D-05	0.16550D-06
120.	0.16049D-04	0.40410D-05	0.16550D-06
130.	0.15905D-04	0.66080D-05	0.16535D-06
135.	0.15840D-04	0.79609D-05	0.16524D-06
150.	0.15680D-04	0.11798D-04	0.16483D-06
165.	0.15579D-04	0.14550D-04	0.16448D-06
180.	0.15545D-04	0.15545D-04	0.16434D-06

ALPHA = 0.08

THETA	SS	PP	SP
0.	0.97318D-04	0.97318D-04	0.81272D-06
5.	0.97280D-04	0.96643D-04	0.81310D-06
10.	0.97165D-04	0.94632D-04	0.81426D-06
20.	0.96712D-04	0.86839D-04	0.81873D-06
30.	0.95970D-04	0.74728D-04	0.82573D-06
40.	0.94964D-04	0.59582D-04	0.83461D-06
45.	0.94371D-04	0.51388D-04	0.83950D-06
50.	0.93724D-04	0.43096D-04	0.84456D-06
60.	0.92287D-04	0.27216D-04	0.85474D-06
70.	0.90698D-04	0.13886D-04	0.86431D-06
80.	0.89004D-04	0.47598D-05	0.87253D-06
90.	0.87256D-04	0.91465D-06	0.87890D-06
100.	0.85509D-04	0.26640D-05	0.88310D-06
110.	0.83815D-04	0.95116D-05	0.88512D-06
120.	0.82225D-04	0.20268D-04	0.88517D-06
130.	0.80789D-04	0.33294D-04	0.88369D-06
135.	0.80141D-04	0.40095D-04	0.88254D-06
150.	0.78542D-04	0.59098D-04	0.87844D-06
165.	0.77537D-04	0.72436D-04	0.87494D-06
180.	0.77194D-04	0.77194D-04	0.87358D-06

P = 0.10   M = 1.40

ALPHA = 0.02

THETA	SS	PP	SP
0.	0.43557D-07	0.43557D-07	0.65927D-09
5.	0.43556D-07	0.43233D-07	0.65928D-09
10.	0.43553D-07	0.42270D-07	0.65931D-09
20.	0.43541D-07	0.38563D-07	0.65941D-09
30.	0.43522D-07	0.32877D-07	0.65956D-09
40.	0.43495D-07	0.25894D-07	0.65974D-09
45.	0.43480D-07	0.22175D-07	0.65983D-09
50.	0.43463D-07	0.18453D-07	0.65992D-09
60.	0.43425D-07	0.11449D-07	0.66008D-09
70.	0.43383D-07	0.57278D-08	0.66017D-09
80.	0.43338D-07	0.19816D-08	0.66020D-09
90.	0.43292D-07	0.66163D-09	0.66013D-09
100.	0.43246D-07	0.19235D-08	0.65998D-09
110.	0.43201D-07	0.56074D-08	0.65974D-09
120.	0.43159D-07	0.11259D-07	0.65944D-09
130.	0.43121D-07	0.18188D-07	0.65910D-09
135.	0.43104D-07	0.21871D-07	0.65893D-09
150.	0.43062D-07	0.32461D-07	0.65845D-09
165.	0.43036D-07	0.40198D-07	0.65811D-09
180.	0.43027D-07	0.43027D-07	0.65799D-09

ALPHA = 0.04

THETA	SS	PP	SP
0.	0.27775D-05	0.27775D-05	0.41289D-07
5.	0.27772D-05	0.27571D-05	0.41291D-07
10.	0.27764D-05	0.26966D-05	0.41298D-07
20.	0.27734D-05	0.24634D-05	0.41324D-07
30.	0.27684D-05	0.21048D-05	0.41363D-07
40.	0.27616D-05	0.16627D-05	0.41409D-07
45.	0.27576D-05	0.14265D-05	0.41433D-07
50.	0.27532D-05	0.11895D-05	0.41456D-07
60.	0.27435D-05	0.74198D-06	0.41495D-07
70.	0.27328D-05	0.37428D-06	0.41521D-07
80.	0.27213D-05	0.13116D-06	0.41526D-07
90.	0.27095D-05	0.41894D-07	0.41510D-07
100.	0.26977D-05	0.11629D-06	0.41470D-07
110.	0.26863D-05	0.34345D-06	0.41409D-07
120.	0.26756D-05	0.69347D-06	0.41331D-07
130.	0.26659D-05	0.11217D-05	0.41245D-07
135.	0.26615D-05	0.13487D-05	0.41201D-07
150.	0.26507D-05	0.19983D-05	0.41079D-07
165.	0.26439D-05	0.24699D-05	0.40992D-07
180.	0.26416D-05	0.26416D-05	0.40961D-07

ALPHA = 0.06

THETA	SS	PP	SP
0.	0.31443D-04	0.31443D-04	0.45314D-06
5.	0.31436D-04	0.31218D-04	0.45320D-06
10.	0.31417D-04	0.30551D-04	0.45337D-06
20.	0.31338D-04	0.27971D-04	0.45404D-06
30.	0.31210D-04	0.23986D-04	0.45504D-06
40.	0.31036D-04	0.19043D-04	0.45623D-06
45.	0.30933D-04	0.16387D-04	0.45684D-06
50.	0.30821D-04	0.13712D-04	0.45742D-06
60.	0.30573D-04	0.86273D-05	0.45843D-06
70.	0.30297D-04	0.44093D-05	0.45908D-06
80.	0.30004D-04	0.15764D-05	0.45923D-06
90.	0.29702D-04	0.46865D-06	0.45879D-06
100.	0.29400D-04	0.11952D-05	0.45777D-06
110.	0.29107D-04	0.36192D-05	0.45620D-06
120.	0.28832D-04	0.73840D-05	0.45423D-06
130.	0.28583D-04	0.11974D-04	0.45202D-06
135.	0.28471D-04	0.14394D-04	0.45089D-06
150.	0.28194D-04	0.21258D-04	0.44776D-06
165.	0.28020D-04	0.26181D-04	0.44554D-06
180.	0.27961D-04	0.27961D-04	0.44474D-06

ALPHA = 0.08

THETA	SS	PP	SP
0.	0.17514D-03	0.17514D-03	0.24110D-05
5.	0.17508D-03	0.17394D-03	0.24116D-05
10.	0.17488D-03	0.17036D-03	0.24133D-05
20.	0.17409D-03	0.15647D-03	0.24200D-05
30.	0.17281D-03	0.13486D-03	0.24300D-05
40.	0.17107D-03	0.10781D-03	0.24418D-05
45.	0.17005D-03	0.93157D-04	0.24479D-05
50.	0.16893D-03	0.78316D-04	0.24538D-05
60.	0.16645D-03	0.49855D-04	0.24638D-05
70.	0.16370D-03	0.25923D-04	0.24703D-05
80.	0.16077D-03	0.95050D-05	0.24718D-05
90.	0.15775D-03	0.25659D-05	0.24675D-05
100.	0.15473D-03	0.56981D-05	0.24572D-05
110.	0.15180D-03	0.18031D-04	0.24416D-05
120.	0.14906D-03	0.37436D-04	0.24219D-05
130.	0.14657D-03	0.60960D-04	0.23998D-05
135.	0.14545D-03	0.73250D-04	0.23886D-05
150.	0.14269D-03	0.10761D-03	0.23573D-05
165.	0.14095D-03	0.13175D-03	0.23351D-05
180.	0.14036D-03	0.14036D-03	0.23270D-05